W9-DAB-630

PRAISE FOR *SIMPLIFY*

"Paul Borthwick is witty and practical as he shares over a hundred ways for us to simplify our overcomplicated lives. This book is meant for everyone, from the consumed business professional to the harried pastor or ministry leader to the overwhelmed parent. You will want to share this book with family and friends."

SAMMY T. MAH, president and CEO of World Relief

"*Simplify* is full of wisdom and wit. . . . Paul Borthwick gives us loads of practical advice on every page to sharpen our focus and create a healthier lifestyle. Make the time to read a most enjoyable and yet challenging book."

JIM BURNS, Ph.D., president of HomeWord and author

"*Simplify*. I can hardly think of a more potent word to speak to harried, hurried people today. And I can hardly imagine a more practical tool than Paul Borthwick's book. He delivers on the title in both style and substance."

BRYAN WILKERSON, senior pastor of Grace Chapel, Lexington, MA

"In the face of confusing and conflicting values in today's secular world we need to reflect on how Christians can make a difference. Paul Borthwick gets to grips with these issues that affect us all and offers examples of how we can put our Christianity to practical use."

RICHARD COLES, former attorney general of the Cayman Islands

SIMPLIFY.

SIMPLIFY.

106 ways to uncomplicate your life

Paul Borthwick

Authentic

COLORADO SPRINGS • LONDON • HYDERABAD

Authentic Publishing
We welcome your questions and comments.

USA   1820 Jet Stream Drive, Colorado Springs, CO 80921
        www.authenticbooks.com
UK   9 Holdom Avenue, Bletchley, Milton Keynes, Bucks, MK1 1QR
        www.authenticmedia.co.uk
India   Logos Bhavan, Medchal Road, Jeedimetla Village, Secunderabad
        500 055, A.P.

Simplify
ISBN-13: 978-1-934068-01-4
ISBN-10: 1-934068-01-2

Cover design: Paul Lewis
Interior design: Angela Lewis
Editorial team: Tom Richards, KJ Larson

Printed in the United States of America

Dedicated to my wife, Christie,

who has been willing to be satisfied with less

so that our lives might be full.

CONTENTS

INTRODUCTION

Do you need this book? Ask yourself before you buy it—lest a book on simplifying your life be added to the cluttered stack of to-be-read literature you already own.

Read this book if you want some help clearing out the clutter of a busy schedule, stressed-out relationships, over-commitments, and a constant sense of being overwhelmed by the volume of choices flying at you every day.

Before proceeding, take a few moments to ask yourself the questions that follow. Do you relate to any of them? If so, then buy this book.

- Are you still working on a two-month-old "To Do" list?

- Could your stack of laundry be declared a national historic site?

- Is a 2-minute microwave meal just not fast enough for you?

- Are you trying to get your five-year-old to learn to use his PDA?

- Do you exhaust yourself on a task only to ask, "Why did I waste my day on that?"

- Is trying to "have it all" leaving you depleted of energy?

- Does your credit card interest on your unpaid balance keep the company in business?

- Do stress headaches drive you to buy aspirin by the case?

- Are your "time-saving devices" actually adding stress to your life?

- Do you sub-consciously hope for a computer virus to give you an excuse for not replying to those 245 unanswered emails?

- Are you too busy to read a book that can help you slow down?

- Are you busier than ever but experiencing less satisfaction?

- Do you suffer from "hurry sickness"—always in a rush to get somewhere but seldom enjoying the moment?

If you answered yes to one or more of these questions, this book is for you, because it is dedicated to providing:

- Practical ideas you can use for daily living;

- Compatible suggestions which can fit into your real world experiences (not some fantasy world designed by someone who has a housekeeper);

- Challenging questions to help you reprioritize and adjust your expectations;

- Enjoyable alternatives to the rat race that help you enjoy the simpler experiences of life;

- Rewarding decisions leading you to personal growth, spiritual refreshment, and family unity;

- Helpful answers in the areas of finances, schedules, technology, and fitness to help you fight back your hectic pace.

A THREE-LEGGED STOOL

This book stands on three basic premises:

Premise One: Many of us are dissatisfied, restless, or overburdened because our lives feel too busy and out-of-control. Even those of us who profess to be followers of Jesus Christ are tired, stressed, and missing the genuine joy we thought would be a natural by-product of living for Him.

Premise Two: The economic realities of our world, where some are extremely affluent and others struggle to survive on one to two dollars per day, combined with our increasing sense of living responsibly in an interdependent Global Village, require that we do some basic rethinking about some of the materialistic goals we pursue and the hectic lifestyles we live.

Premise Three: The combination of premise one and two means that we all face choices—a key to simplifying our lives, restoring a sense of sanity to each day, and living more compatibly with God's design for us in the world.

> This day I call heaven and earth as witnesses against you that I have set before you life and death, blessings and curses. Now choose life, so that you and your children may live and that you may love

the LORD your God, listen to His voice, and hold fast to him. (Deuteronomy 30:19–20)

CHAPTER 1

OVER-CHOICE MEANS STRESSED OUT

One hundred years ago, "burned out" referred to the campfire. "Chronic fatigue syndrome" occurred only in insomniacs. People described an automobile on ice as being "out of control," but they wouldn't refer to their lives that way.

Times change. Our lives get cluttered.

As we face an ever-increasing pace of life governed by email, instant messaging, and 24–7 busyness, we are living out what Alvin Toffler identified as the "age of over-choice." An article in *USA Today* dramatically summarized the staggering number of choices we face every day. According to the article:

- Dreyers Ice Cream offered 34 flavors in 1977; they sell 250 today.

- Arby's, which offered one sandwich in 1964 when it was founded, now offers more than 30, most of which aren't even roast beef.

- Starbucks offers 19,000 ways to get coffee including five types of milk—whole, non-fat, half and half, organic, and soy. You choose sizes, foam or no foam, three types of artificial sweetener, and even extra hot (180 degrees versus 150–170)

- When Whole Foods opened in 1974, it sold two kinds of lettuce; now it sells 40. Its stores sell 15 kinds of mushrooms, many of which weren't sold in the USA five years ago.

- Frito Lay started with two chips—Frito's corn chips and Lay's potato chips—now it has 60, and there are 24 varieties of the Lay's potato chip.

- Tropicana even sells orange juice with three consistencies of pulp.[1]

We face so many options that we may find our-selves paralyzed looking at the options. The resul-tant stress leads us to spend billions of dollars visiting therapists who help us manage our stress and billions more buying headache medications, stomach remedies, and relaxants when the thera-pist cannot dispel the tension within.

> We are surrounded by numerous op-tions. Gathered around each of us is a massive array of alternatives. Some must be done, others can be put off. Some are bad. Others are good. Some tend to deceive us. Others try to moti-vate us. And the supply is ever increas-ing—tending to overwhelm us. We are over-stimulated, overchallenged, overex-posed. And if we don't watch out, we can become over-committed.[2]

Consider television. I am what sociologists call a "Baby Boomer" (born in 1954, I'm part of a mass of people born between 1946 and 1964, the "boom" following World War II). When I was

1. "You Want It Your Way," *USA Today* (March 5–7 edition, 2004), 1–2.

2. J. Grant Howard, *Balancing Life's Demands* (Portland: Multnomah, 1983), 19.

a child, our family purchased our first TV. In those days, there were three network stations in Boston, and I think they signed on at 6 a.m. and off at midnight. As a teenager, UHF stations were introduced. The choices of TV stations doubled, and several channels went to twenty-four hour programming.

In the late 1970s cable TV was added, then it was direct TV, then satellite TV, then movies-on-demand, and on it goes. With the right cable subscription, I can now change channels every minute and, if my home has the average cable service (with more than 150 channels, it will take me almost three hours to return to the channel where I started). Cable TV epitomizes over-choice!

DOWNSIZING OUR OPTIONS

Each person carries a backpack of choices. As we hike into life, we add more and more to that backpack—choices about which car to buy, who to marry, where to live, and which career to pursue. And on it goes. Gradually, our backpacks become so overloaded that we tip over backward onto them—our arms and legs flailing in the air like an overturned beetle trying to right itself. Eventually, our only option is to dump some stuff.

ARE WE CARRYING TOO MUCH?

Mark Littleton summarizes our cluttered lives by identifying these root causes:

- Too many desirable activities beckoning for your attention;

- Too many important choices to make every day;

- Too much information coming at you;

- Too many voices calling for your attention;

- Too many things you want and can have, at the swipe of a credit card;

- Too many advertisers telling you what's important;

- Too many entertaining entertainments;

- Too many things that we "need" to function well;

- Too many tempting temptations;

- Too much guilt.[3]

---

3.   Mark Littleton, *Escaping the Time Crunch* (Chicago: Moody Press, 1990), 44.

Root causes lead to symptoms where over-choice has started to paralyze us. Some of the symptoms of a cluttered life include:

Inability to make commitments. My friend pastors a church primarily made up of young professionals, many of whom remain unmarried into their mid-thirties. In studying their busy lives and minimal activity at church, he observed, "It's hard to have a ministry with people whose primary goal is keeping their options open." Commitment becomes fluid—sticking with one option only until something better comes along. And when something appears better, commitments are shifted like pressing a remote control to change stations.

Inability to decide which choices really matter. Multiple options swamp us so we cannot distinguish the important from the mundane. Gail MacDonald tells the story of a missionary returning to the United States after serving four years in a developing country. When asked about her greatest reentry shock, she replied, "The potato chip aisle." For her, over-choice was most vividly reflected by the variety of chips available at the supermarket. "My friends aren't even aware of the energy it's taking. They've gotten so used to the subtle enslavement. You ask, what has shocked me? It's seeing the time wasted over potato chip decisions, so that when the truly important is-sues need our attention, our energies have been squandered on trivia."[4]

When multiple demands stuff our schedules and options overload our mental circuits, we lose our ability to think clearly. We give ourselves to mulling over potato chips, video rentals, or TV stations—so that when we face important deci-sions, we have no decision-making energy left.

Inability to relax or get quiet. In *Little House on the Freeway*, Tim Hansel lists these characteristics as part of the "OOC (out-of-control) Syndrome."[5] Whether we're trying to multi-task with multiple programs whirring on our computers, or we're trying to watch two television shows at once or we're signing up for more activities at church than we could possibly attend, overstressed lives are noisy lives. We live for the next choice rather than enjoy the moment.

> So you've got the career, the cars, the spouse, the spa, the house, the health club, the kids, and the clothes. Trouble is you're so frantic, frazzled, overbooked,

---

4.　Gail MacDonald, *Keep Climbing* (Wheaton: Tyndale, 1989), 29.

5.　Tim Hansel, *Little House on the Freeway* (Portland: Multnomah, 1987), 17–28.

and overwhelmed you don't have time to enjoy any of it.[6]

One author offers a contemporary contrast to Psalm 23 which reflects our contemporary spirit of stress.

Psalm 23, Antithesis

The clock is my dictator, I shall not rest.
It makes me lie down only when exhausted.
It leads me to deep depression.
It hounds my soul.
It leads me in circles of frenzy for activity's sake.
Even though I run frantically from task to task,
I will never get it all done, for my "ideal" is with me.
Deadlines and my need for approval, they drive me.
They demand my performance from me, beyond
the limits of my schedule.
They anoint my head with migraines.
My in-basket overflows.
Surely fatigue and time pressure shall follow me
all the days of my life,
And I will dwell in the bonds of frustration
forever.[7]

---

6.   Claudia Morgan, "The Stress of Having It All," *Washington Post* (September 22, 1988), C5.

7.   Marcia K. Hornok, Discipleship Journal, (Issue 60 1990), 23. Used by permission. All rights reserved.

Constant feelings of dissatisfaction, David Johnson, a pastor on Cape Cod, Massachusetts, observes a growing number of experience junkies in the church. These people, always in search of a new experience (even in Christian work), hope that the next one adventure or "extreme" something will bring the rush of happiness that has eluded them.

They become like the fanatic, who, unsure of his direction, doubles his speed. Jacks of all trades and masters of none, they pursue new and varied options in hopes of finding satisfaction. Instead, they experience the law of diminishing returns—each new selection less pleasing. After innumerable experiences, people walk away tired, bored, and disillusioned.

Lots of activity but little focus. There's an old story of the farmer who went out hunting with his hound dog.

> When the farmer returned, he still seemed fresh, but the dog flopped down on the porch, exhausted. Someone asked him what was wrong, and he said, "Well, it wasn't the walking. We only covered ten miles. But there wasn't a gate open along the way that he didn't go

in and examine the whole field. Not a cat appeared but that he had to chase it—rabbits too. And there wasn't a dog barked but that he wore himself out barking back and showing fight. He must have gone fifty miles to my ten. No, it weren't the route that got him, but the zigzagging."[8]

Lack of focus often manifests itself in multitasking that results in unfinished projects. We begin a project, finish about 50 to 75 percent of it, and then lay it aside to pursue a new interest. The project sits for days, weeks, or even months as a testimony to our lack of focus. Sally McClung writes, "We need to finish what we start. Unfinished tasks waste our time and drain our mental peace. Even the woodpecker owes his success to the fact that he uses his head and keeps pecking away until he finishes the job he starts."[9]

Many of us are busier than ever, but if we are willing to do some honest evaluation, we will have to admit we waste a lot of energy zigzagging— exhausting ourselves with less-than-purposeful activities.

---

8. Mark Littleton, 230–31.

9. Sally McClung, *Where Will I Find the Time?* (Eugene: Harvest House, 1989), 90.

THERE IS HOPE!

Feeling burdened? Overstressed? Documenting lives burdened by over-choice is easy. But what do we do about it? When it comes to multiple choices, we face three options.

Rich chose to quit. He conceded the battle by withdrawing into an easier world, abandoning his family and friends in stressed-out Los Angeles and moving to a less cluttered life on a Caribbean island. (Others like Rich choose places like the backwoods of Maine or the wilds of Nome, Alaska instead.) He wanted to simplify life, and he saw no other option than to run from his commitments.

People without as much courage or resources retire more subtly. They resort to drugs, alcohol, television, the Internet, computer games, or some other distraction in an effort to achieve the mental numbness which provides the escape they desire from option overload.

Diane chose to "go with the flow," bobbing through life like a cork on the ocean, making as few selections as possible and simply allowing circumstances to determine her choices. Over-choice in her case led to irresponsibility. She thought, "I can't cope with the choices, so I will become a pawn in a chess game played by others."

In Diane's case, even God got blamed. "I am just waiting on God" is one of her favorite lines. But in her case, waiting on God became synonymous with a passive approach to life. Choosing not to decide became her decision.

My wife, Christie, and I have chosen to choose. We have busy, stress-filled lives. We look at our cluttered lives, and we make decisions based on our conviction: "This is not the way we think God wants us to live." So we make choices regularly throughout the year. We try to make choices that reflect:

- A God-centered pace-of-life in our contemporary times.

- Pro-active steps to manage our clutter rather than allowing it to manage us.

- Biblical values for Christians who are relating to a global cultural reality, not simply the American way of life.

- Our biblical hope that we can, through personal choice, learn to simplify our lives to become more purposeful and enjoyable.

- The scriptural mandate to "choose life" (Deuteronomy 30:19)—to invest our resources in life rather than in possessions, in *being* rather than *having*.

- Focused lives. Rather than fragment ourselves in a dozen different directions, we attempt to recognize both our opportunities and limitations and ask where we can make the greatest impact for God.

Such steps have never come easy (at this writing, we're approaching 30 years of marriage). We instinctively resist tough and limiting choices because, in the words of Haddon Robinson, "Many people don't want to make good decisions; they want to make painless decisions."[10]

In *The Seven Habits of Highly Effective People,* Stephen Covey identifies being proactive as the first habit he observed in people he studied. We decided to be proactive with respect to our choices. The choices we focused on are reflected in this book.

THANK GOD FOR THE OPTIONS

The world's poorest people do not generally suffer from over-choice. The essence of being poor is not having choices. When survival be-

---

10. Haddon Robinson, *Decision Making by the Book* (Wheaton: Victor Books, 1991), 90.

comes the daily priority for the world's two billion people who live on less than two dollars per day,[11] choosing an outfit to wear or which restaurant for dinner becomes irrelevant. So thank God for choices. The fact that we even have choices to make indicates we are far better off than many people in our world.

But perhaps we have overdone it. Most of us would gladly relinquish some of the stresses associated with our multi-choice lives because answering "all of the above" is simply not possible. We thank God for the choices—most of us would not choose the simpler life of the world's poor—but sometimes our lives get cluttered with over-choice.

So what then? Shall we return to earlier times, like life two hundred years ago? I doubt it. Who wants to return to a time without cars or central heating, where marriages were arranged, and children died of measles? The good ol' days might disappoint us.

But advances in technology and lifestyle continue to increase our choices. We face choices

---

11. Estimates range from 2 to 3 billion of the earth's 6+ billion live on $1 to $2 per day. See United Nations data cited at http://www.geocities.com/socialistpartynortheastbranch/tdtas

that our predecessors never encountered, and, after thanking God for the options we have, we still need to choose.

This is a book about choices—choices each of us can make to dump some stuff from our allegorical backpacks of life so that we can right ourselves for the hike ahead.

WAYS TO SIMPLIFY
YOUR LIFE

1. Adopt an "environmental impact" statement

1

ADOPT AN "ENVIRONMENTAL IMPACT" STATEMENT

"Environmental impact" describes the impact one action has upon another—specifically related to the environment. Will building that bridge alter the marine life on the shore of the river? How will the emissions from a factory alter the air quality of the surrounding community? Developers and builders are forced to deal with the unintended potentially negative consequences before moving ahead.

In the same way, we need to realize that choices we make come with corresponding impact on other areas of our lives—beyond the immediate choice. Before making any of the choices referred to in the next 105 suggestions, do your own "environmental impact" study on each choice you make. In the case of adding new functions to your life, ask yourself, "What do I need to adjust or delete to make time available for this?"

For example, before making the decision to simplify family life by trying to live with one car rather than two, discuss whether or not the decision will really ease or create more stress—especially when looking at the long-term family schedule.

For most of us, the problem is not making choices; the problem is underestimating the impact of those choices. A larger house may seem wise for a growing family, but it might mean more cleaning, higher taxes, bigger mortgages, and increased yard work. Cutting back on coffee consumption may be the right thing to do, but it may mean headaches or sluggishness for several days or even a week. Thus, planning when to cut back is as important as deciding to cut back.

We all need to simplify. Studying the impact of choices on our personal environment can help us make long-lasting cutbacks.

CHAPTER 2

DISCERNING WANT VERSUS NEED

It possessed me as I sat in my living room. I think it was about 9:40 p.m. I was minding my own business, relaxing in front of a favorite TV show. Suddenly, a hunger came over me; I felt this incredible urge to call for a pizza to be delivered. The power drove me to the Yellow Pages. I picked up the phone and dialed the first few numbers.

Suddenly, I realized: Wait a minute. I will retire in about an hour, and I seldom eat this late—especially pizza. I don't even like home-delivered pizza; it's greasy and expensive. And I don't need any more food; I had a good meal about three hours ago. I hung up the phone.

What happened? Was it the evil pizza spirit from which I needed to be delivered? Had I disliked my dinner, and my urge for pizza was revealing a secret desire that I had repressed?

It was nothing so complicated. It was effective advertising at work. A television commercial sent me a message—a luscious-looking pizza could be mine in minutes. If I dialed a certain number, I too could soon be enjoying my cheese treasure. Order now and I could be as happy as the people on the commercial.

OPTION BOMBARDMENT

Every day in thousands of different ways, advertisements assault our conscious and unconscious thoughts. These ads tell us what to do to be:

- More beautiful, handsome, or youthful,

- More popular or successful,

- More effective parents or more attractive singles,

- More connected electronically,

- Or simply happier and more fulfilled.

The multiple demands we respond to in the media provide one of the major sources of clutter and stress in our lives. It comes through TV, Internet pop-up ads, magazines, shopping networks, catalogs, bulk mail, billboards, and newspapers. And if we miraculously escape these images, we could still find ourselves being solicited by sales people telephoning to sell us subscriptions, vinyl siding for our homes, or new credit cards.

All of this is designed to create either a sense of need or dissatisfaction with what we already have. The most effective use images and phrases designed to encourage us to act without thinking. Producers want us to feel hungry so that we will consume. They appeal to what Bill Hybels identifies as the Monster called "More." Craig Blomberg, author of *Neither Poverty nor Riches: a Biblical Theology of Material Possessions* writes:

It is arguable that materialism is the single biggest competitor with authentic Christianity for the hearts and souls of millions in our world today, including many in the visible church.[1]

1. Craig Blomberg, *Neither Poverty nor Riches: A Biblical Theology of Material Possessions,* (Downers Grove, IL: Inter Varsity Press, 2001), 132.

And if we do not feel pressured to buy something, we feel obliged to do something. The media reminds me that I never seem to exercise enough, vacation enough, or work around the house enough.

One interesting exercise in discernment involves comparing advertising against the three motives to sin found in 1 John 2:15–16 (NAS): the lust of the eyes, the lust of the flesh, and the boastful pride of life. The "lust of the flesh" certainly fueled the pizza commercial that almost started me towards the late-night binge. Everything in it spoke to physical cravings. The "lust of the eyes" can draw our attention to ads for automobiles, perfume, jewels, and other material possessions: if I own that new lawnmower, I'll be the envy of the neighborhood. The "boastful pride of life" appeals to everything selfish in us. I'm worth it. My worth somehow increases if I can drive the ultimate driving machine.

A BIBLICAL RESPONSE

So what do we do? We live in the West, part of what one person called the "R.M.C. Block"—Rich,

Materialistic Countries.[2] In our world, our expectations about possessions and comforts have increased to the point that:

- Want has become need.

- Luxury has become necessity.

- And optional features have become standard equipment.

- And even if we don't need it, we can justify anything by waiting until it goes on sale.[3]

Harvard University professor Juliet Schor did a landmark study on "the unexpected decline of leisure" entitled *The Overworked American: Why We Want What We Don't Need.*[4] In it, she summarized her findings that people were working harder, longer hours. The reason? To get more! In a follow-up study five years later, *The Overspent American,*[5] she documents the exponential growth of material expectations and how it has led to overwork and increased indebtedness.

---

2. Larry Brook, "Make a Prophet?" *Interlit* (June, 1991); 23.

3. George Murray, in an address entitled "Fanning Your Spiritual Fire" at the ACMC National Conference, Wheaton, Illinois, July 19, 1991.

4. Juliet Schor, *The Overworked American: Why We Want What We Don't Need,* (New York, NY: HarperCollins) 1999.

5. Ibid.

In this world, Proverbs 30:7–9 provides sane, biblical guidelines to discern want versus need and deliver us from the stress and clutter advertisers force on us:

Two things I ask of you, O LORD; do not refuse me before I die:

Keep falsehood and lies far from me;

Give me neither poverty nor riches, but give me only my daily bread.

Otherwise, I may have too much and disown you and say, 'Who is the LORD?'

Or I may become poor and steal, and so dishonor the name of my God.

Neither poverty nor riches—because one leads to desperate measures such as stealing, and the other leads to arrogant self-reliance. Either extreme inhibits a right relationship with God. In a society where want is sometimes perceived as need, we may have to practice discernment to know the difference.[6]

---

6. Craig Blomberg, *Neither Poverty nor Riches: A Biblical Theology of Material Possessions*, (Downers Grove, IL: Inter Varsity Press) takes off from these verses to give a healthy and balanced overview of material possessions and wealth related to the people of the Bible.

QUESTIONS TO BUILD DISCERNMENT

Our goal in simplifying our lives is to grow in discernment so that we make wiser choices with our time, our money, and our relationships. But discernment takes practice. The writer to the Hebrews reminds us that maturity means training ourselves to distinguish good from evil (see Hebrews 5:14).

In his book, *The Pursuit of Holiness,* Jerry Bridges offers some excellent questions designed to help us exercise our discernment muscles. His "Formula: How to Know Right from Wrong" builds on three verses in 1 Corinthians. Each question in the formula helps us pause—to gain discernment—before purchasing something new or signing up for a "great opportunity."

- "Everything is permissible for me—but not everything is beneficial" (1 Corinthians 6:12).

  QUESTION 1: Is it helpful physically, spiritually, and mentally? Using my pizza commercial encounter, the answer would be no. Pizza before bedtime gives me indigestion and hinders restful sleep.

- "Everything is permissible for me—but I will not be mastered by anything" (1 Corinthians 6:12).

  QUESTION 2: Does it bring me under its power? Was I going to order that pizza because I had given it some thought or because I was being impulsively mastered by the commercial?

- "Therefore, if what I eat causes my brother to fall into sin, I will never eat meat again, so that I will not cause him to fall" (1 Corinthians 8:13).

  QUESTION 3: Does it hurt others? In my pizza experience, the question might not apply, unless, of course, Christie was already asleep. In that case, I would have hurt her either by having a pizza party without her or (more realistically) by using our spending money impulsively and irresponsibly.

- "So whether you eat or drink or whatever you do, do it all for the glory of God" (1 Corinthians 10:31).

QUESTION 4: Does it glorify God?[7] Pizza at 10 p.m.? I doubt it.

EVALUATING EXPECTATIONS

I spoke to the Singles Fellowship at our church about dealing with disappointments, a topic they had chosen. After the message (we studied the life of Joseph, who dreamed of greatness but got the pit, servanthood, and a prison cell instead), I asked one of the coordinators why they had chosen this topic. He replied, "Because the vast number of attendees feels that life is not turning out as they had expected."

Dashed expectations lead to disappointment, and disappointment creates voids which we try to fill (or others try to fill for us). Part of the reason advertisers succeed stems from our expectations—we want happiness and we want it now! Most of us raised in the affluent countries of the Western world are considered children of privilege. We hold a "sense of entitlement"—that a good life with a successful lifestyle (or at least

---

7.   Jerry Bridges, *The Pursuit of Holiness* (Colorado Springs: NavPress, 1978), 91.

a lifestyle better than our parents had) is something we deserve.

Adjusting to modern life means modifying our expectations. We must learn to say no and bring our expectations in line with reality. The "American Dream" lifestyle—if it ever existed—costs too much in money, broken relationships, and time. Living with unrealistic and overinflated expectations does not work. We know we need to simplify, but simplifying means adjusting the expectations that launched us into adulthood.

Christie invented a phrase that helps us. One day while we were looking at some sort of new household gadgets, I asked Christie if she wanted something. "No," she responded, "my house is full." That phrase—"my house is full"—has helped us say no to things—even nice, desirable, on-sale, everybody-has-one things. We say no because left unchecked, our expectations can become our master. Tom Sine succinctly summarized, "Whatever commands our time, energy, and resources, commands us."[8]

8.　Tom Sine, "Will the Real Cultural Christians Please Stand Up?" *World Vision* (October/November1989): 21.

To start trimming expectations, cutting back on spending, decreasing our unwise use of resources, and modifying our lifestyles to a sane balance, consider the following.

WAYS TO SIMPLIFY YOUR LIFE

2. Buy slowly

3. Resist temptation

4. Adjust without overdoing it

5. Don't fit in

6. Beware the "want-makers"

7. Challenge your terminology

8. Think categorically

9. Stay out of debt

10. Define your limits

11. Define your "real" needs

12. Watch for ways to save money

13. Don't buy on impulse

14. Remember the lasting secret of accumulating wealth

15. Make a list

16. Eat before food shopping

17. Simplify and serve

18. Know your priorities

19. Don't fuel covetousness

20. Give it away

21. Toss that mail

22. Pinch yourself

2

BUY SLOWLY

When considering any major purchase, wait. Pausing before we purchase can keep us from buying on a whim, which is one of the causes of credit card debt in our country. Credit cards give us an illusionary buying power, and purchasing things over the Internet or through catalogs serve our impulses ("see it; like it; buy it").

If our credit card statement tells us that we have $5,000 in available credit, we can spend $5,000, right? Buying slowly keeps us from being duped into thinking that "plastic" and real money are synonymous. An interesting note here: A major credit card advertisement touts the slogan "Master the Possibilities." What it fails to explain, however, is that using any card without forethought or planning may result in the debts mastering us. Remember Paul's words in 1 Corinthians 6:12: "I will not be mastered by anything."

3

RESIST TEMPTATION

An article in a local paper described customers at a local "bargain" store as *"People Shopping for Things to Need."* Stay away from shopping centers or malls except when you have a specific purchase in mind. Don't surf the Internet gazing at all the stuff for sale on eBay or at the website of your favorite clothing, technology, music, or DVD store. Window-shopping in all forms induces buying. That's why professionals spend so much time decorating the windows, jazzing up their websites, and bombarding your Christmas mail with catalogs.

4

ADJUST WITHOUT OVERDOING IT

Evaluate what things we need to serve effectively in our culture (i.e., so you don't stick out like an oddity) against purchases or amenities advertisers tell us we must have to be acceptable.

In the business world, for example, nicer clothes are often a requirement that enables the business person to function effectively. We might accept this as part of professional survival, but there is no need to buy designer labels at top prices. In my experience, no one has ever turned down the collar of my shirt to see which label I wear and stated: "Ha! I knew it! Borthwick's label is fake; he's wearing a knock-off. And we deal only with men who wear Ralph Lauren originals."

5

DON'T FIT IN

Identify distinctively non-Christian cultural values, and aggressively make a choice not to fit in. If cheating is common-place in business dealings, or if normal practice is to get clients drunk over three-martini lunches before presenting the sale, we who follow Jesus Christ must resist and live by His truth.

6

BEWARE THE "WANT-MAKERS"

While browsing through the library, I was in the non-fiction section looking at the titles in the business section. I had benefitted in the past from books on being organized and developing and living by priorities, so I was scanning the titles.

I came across a book entitled *The Want Makers.*[9] The title caught my eye so I took it back to my desk to peruse its contents. It was a book on advertising. The basic premise? Advertising is creating want in people for things they don't need. I was amazed because the book was neither apologizing nor rationalizing related to issues of selling people useless products. It was simply written to tell business people that success in sales means spinning the facts about a product in such a way that people will buy—even if they have no need of it.

When I asked a friend involved in advertising about the book, he joked, "My job is *convincing people to buy things they don't need with money they don't have.*" The advertiser's comment and the title of that book is a reminder. Every commercial or written advertisement that touches your senses every day is designed to create

9.   Eric Clarke, *The Want-Makers* (London: Hodder and Stoughton, 1989).

want or desire in you. Financial advisor Dave Ramsey observed:

> We live in the most aggressively marketed-to culture in the history of the world. We have more advertising impressions fly in front of our faces in one month than the average person had in a year and a half in 1954 . . . and the most aggressively marketed product is debt, with five billion credit card offers in our mailboxes in 2005.[10]

Let the marketed-to beware!

---

10. Dave Ramsey, author of *The Total Money Makeover*, in an interview with John Carroll, "Debt Man Talking," *American Way Magazine* (December 1, 2006), 35.

7

CHALLENGE YOUR TERMINOLOGY

After we meet our basic needs, almost everything should be identified as a want. Several years ago, we decided we *needed* a new car. Then I read in a newspaper article that only 8 percent of the people on earth own cars.[11] With that in mind, we could not buy another car based on "need."

8

THINK CATEGORICALLY

Try to categorize things as valid wants (i.e., a dishwasher for a family of five) ver-sus luxuries (a speedboat used only for

---

11. "Travel Tidbits," *Boston Globe*, September 22, 1991: B3.

water-skiing). One of the great traps of adulthood is our ability to convince ourselves that very expensive toys are needs.

9

STAY OUT OF DEBT

If you don't have the cash available or know immediately where it is coming from, think first before swiping that credit card. Ask first, "How will we pay for this purchase if we use our credit cards?" Credit card debt is a killer and often leads to living at 110 percent of our annual income. An estimated 43 percent of American consumers spend more than they earn each year.[12]

Proverbs 22:7 reminds us that the borrower becomes the lender's slave. Indebtedness gives someone or something else the capacity to dictate our priorities.

---

12. Kim Khan, "How does your debt compare?" http://moneycentral.msn.com/content/SavingandDebt/P70581.asp

Data from 2004 states that the average household has more than $8,000 in credit card debt, up from about $3,000 in 1990. An $8,000 debt at a rate of 18 percent interest will take more than 25 years to repay and cost more than $24,000.[13]

This debt, in turn, produces stress in our marriages, demands we work harder and longer, and limits our giving to those in real need (see Proverbs 22:7; Romans 13:8).

Note: For those strapped by debt and mismanaged finances, resources available through the "Good Sense" ministry of the Willow Creek Association can be very helpful.[14]

---

13. Ibid.

14. http://www.willowcreek.org/GoodSense/resources.asp

10

DEFINE YOUR LIMITS

Determine the base amount you need to live and stay within those limits. Then, when you receive unplanned income, you can invest in special ministries or a long-term financial plan.

Ajith Fernando, pastor and Youth for Christ leader in Sri Lanka, has written several books, but he challenged my "life within limits" when he told me that he determined to live on his salary alone and give all of the proceeds from his book royalties to help others in the ministry. Rather than expanding his lifestyle to fit the income, he controlled his lifestyle by limiting his income.

Bill Hybels, pastor of Willow Creek Community Church, teaches that we should give 10 percent, save 10 percent, and live on 80 percent of our income—a marked contrast to what the credit card companies tell us.

11

DEFINE YOUR "REAL" NEEDS

When you identify a true need—for instance, education, clothing, or a car—evaluate your limits. What type of car will you need? What are your clothing needs? Remember, advertisers and credit card companies will encourage you to live beyond your means.

When Christie went back to school, we looked into a home equity line of credit, a loan that borrows against the equity in our home. Before we applied however, we sought advice from a financial counselor because we had heard of people losing their homes by misusing this kind of credit.

We asked, "Before we sign off on this thing, tell us how we can avoid serious trouble." The adviser explained that some people take home equity lines of credit to consolidate their debt—let's assume $10,000. They borrow $10,000 against the equity in their home to pay off maxed-out credit cards. They start getting credit card statements offering $10,000 in available credit, so they start charging again, forgetting the $10,000 borrowed on their home. Net result: they end up doubling their debt rather than consolidating it.

It's better to define your limits beforehand.

12

WATCH FOR WAYS TO SAVE MONEY

Pray and shop for bargains: clothes marked "second" are often more than adequate. When I started work at the church, I knew I needed a nice suit for Sunday services. I also knew we had little available money for such a purchase.

So we prayed and went off to look for a suit at a thrift store. As we rummaged through the clothes in (or near) my size, we came across a beautiful Pierre Cardin suit. I tried it on; it looked tailor-made for me. The cost: $29.00.

Remember the bargain shopper's motto: Everything will eventually go on sale. Warning: Discount outlets and bargain basements can be a blessing and a curse. On one hand, they sell "seconds" or designer labels for less, reducing our clothing costs. On the other hand, bargains can create a destructive, materialistic attitude.

My wife Christie is an avid saver and bargain hunter. She bought her wedding gown for $25, paid $79 to get it cleaned and voila! A wedding gown for just over $100! We saved money there and used it for a little nicer honeymoon. More importantly, she helped establish a marriage spending pattern that has taken us through almost 30 years of marriage.

Christie works at a hospital, and every day she has a couple of breaks where she enjoys a cup of tea. She now brings her own tea bags because the hospital cafeteria gives free cups and hot water, but you pay for the tea bag. She calculated that she saves over $300/year on tea bags alone, and $300 goes a long way in other parts of the world. It's an example, but it makes the point.

13

DON'T BUY ON IMPULSE

"Through presumption comes nothing but strife." Ask yourself before you make a purchase, "Can I survive without it?" Or, "How have we survived up to this point without it?" Other questions to ask might include:

- What brought the item into consideration: did I seek it or just see it?

- How long will it be useful?

- Is there a cheaper alternative?

- What advice do I get from others about this purchase? (Consumer Reports gives good, objective help, especially on major purchases.)

14

REMEMBER THE LASTING SECRET OF ACCUMULATING WEALTH

In our community, a number of families have come from other countries, and they amaze their neighbors by their ability to purchase homes within their first few years of being in the country. What makes this most amazing is that homes in our community often sell for $750,000 to $2 million dollars (we purchased our home in 1984, long before the real estate prices skyrocketed for those readers who are wondering).

I befriended one of these families who had come from Hong Kong. In a conversation with the father of the family, I asked him how they did it. My friend's name is Mr. Tan. I asked, "Mr. Tan, you have purchased a home very quickly, and you told me that you bought the home without going into debt. Can you tell me the secret of

Chinese wealth?" I say with my note pad ready and pen in hand.

He responded quickly and briefly: "We spend less than we make."

That was it. In six words, he gave perhaps the best financial advice anyone can get: live below your means. If you make more money than you spend, you'll always have excess, you'll be able to save for important future purchases; you'll be able to be more generous; and you'll sleep better at night.

15

MAKE A LIST

A person with a list, who has thought through purchases before leaving the house and then sets out to buy what is planned, is less likely to buy unnecessary items than someone else who says, "Let's just go walk around and see what I might need." In addition, list-making can help us make the most efficient use of time. Planning ahead helps consolidate purchasing; a random approach often results in multiple errands.

16

EAT BEFORE FOOD SHOPPING

Shopping on an empty stomach results in junk food or other unnecessary purchases.

17

SIMPLIFY AND SERVE

"Live more simply that others may simply live." This means cutting back so that someone poorer can benefit. Skipping a meal once a week and sending the money saved to hunger relief (an idea that comes right out of Isaiah 58:6–10) has been adopted by many families. One family stopped cluttering their family time with cable TV. They canceled their subscription and donated the money to support an orphan through World Vision.

In this regard, we try to think in terms "dynamic equivalents" with our money. For example, before spending money on some optional item, we ask, "What *else* could that same amount of money buy?" Do you know that money spent buying CD's, downloading music, or subscribing to cable movie channels could support a child through World Vision or Compassion Project?[15] We calculated a few years ago that we were spending over $1000/year in eating at restaurants or fast food places. That same amount can support full-time

15. World Vision child sponsorship is (at this writing) $35/month (www.worldvision.org). Compassion International child sponsorship is (at this writing) $32/month (http://www.compassion.com/sponsor_a_child/default.htm).

Christian workers in many parts of the world.[16]

18

KNOW YOUR PRIORITIES

No one "has it all." Adjusting priorities means that an inferior value is sacrificed for a superior one. Norm and Debbie had been discussing how they wanted their yard to look. Their image of a *Better Homes and Gardens* landscape presented a problem. They had three children under age ten. One day Debbie called out to Norm to stop their son from digging up the lawn. Norm responded with something he'd heard on James Dobson's radio program: "But, honey, we're raising kids here—not grass." Norm understood his priorities. A beautiful lawn would have to wait.

---

16. A good source of information in sponsoring international Christian workers is Partners International (www.partnersintl.org).

19

DON'T FUEL COVETOUSNESS

Don't watch shopping networks or television shows—or subscribe to magazines—that create "the lust of the eyes, the lust of the flesh, or the boastful pride of life" (see 1 John 2:15–17). Obviously, this includes pornography, which is designed to make us want something we cannot have. But it's also true of certain TV shows and any manner of other visual imagery that make us dissatisfied with what we have, covetous of others, and prone to spend beyond our means.

20 ———————

GIVE IT AWAY

Go through your house looking for things you consider useless that could help someone less fortunate.

Go through the closet and give away clothes you have not worn in a long time or may never wear again.

Donate useful (but unused) furnishings and appliances cluttering your attic and basement. From thrift store revenues, the Salvation Army funds many of its urban outreaches to the poor or alcohol-dependent.

Take the family to serve a holiday meal at a soup kitchen. It builds thankfulness, teaches you and your children to serve without reciprocation, and suppresses those self-indulgent tendencies that surface during the holidays.

21

TOSS THAT MAIL

Don't spend too much time reading junk mail telling you to buy, give, go, or do—all on impulse. It's better to be proactive, deciding ahead of time how you will use your time and money, than react to someone else's priorities.

22

PINCH YOURSELF

C.S. Lewis, writing about charitable giving, encouraged every Christian to live more simply:

> If our expenditure on comforts, luxuries, amusements, etc. is up to the standard common among those with the same income as our own, we are probably giving away too

little. If our charities do not at all pinch or hamper us, I should say they are too small. There ought to be things we should like to do and cannot do because our charitable expenditures exclude them.[17]

---

17. C.S. Lewis, *Mere Christianity* (New York: Macmillan, 1958), 81–82.

CHAPTER 3

STAYING FIT

"So how do you look at life—like a TV dinner or as a chicken pot pie? Do you segment your life into the physical, spiritual, intellectual, economic, etc., like separated portions of that TV dinner? Or do you see all of life as a spiritual mix, with each ingredient affecting the others, like chicken pot pie?"

The speaker, Dr. Bingham Hunter, challenged our congregation to evaluate their overview of the Christian life, and his challenge provides a pivotal point (food) as we evaluate physical fitness.

Most of us (at least those who think in the "TV dinner" category) seldom think physical fitness or eating habits have a direct correlation to our spiritual lives. With the possible exception of cigarette smoking, illegal drugs, or alcohol, most of us ignore the connection between physical and spiritual health.

But the Bible (which presents more of a "chicken pot pie" view of life) connects our bodies and spirits. Fasting and spiritual intensity go hand in hand—see Matthew 6:18 or Isaiah 58:1–10. Our physical posture (kneeling or prostrating oneself, for example) reminds us of our dependence on God (Luke 18:18; Revelation 1:17). Exhaustion and spiritual depression have a reciprocal relationship—see 1 Kings 19:1–9.

Ironically, the New Age movement, which most Christians discount as a deviation of Hinduism applied to Western society, has drawn many followers by teaching holistic health—body, mind, and spirit. They err in their focus, looking inward rather than to Jesus for spiritual reality, but the concept is fundamentally correct. Body, soul, and spirit do connect.

Michael Quoist explains the relationship:

> If your body makes all the decisions and gives all the orders, and if you obey, the physical effectively destroys every other dimension of your personality. Your

emotional life will be blunted and your spiritual life will be stifled and ultimately will become anemic.[1]

As Christians, our physical habits and spiritual priorities need evaluating. How can we change our diets, our exercise, our physical pace, and our perspective to enhance health and spiritual alertness?

MY PERSONAL TESTIMONY

I never cared for discussions about health food—roughage, cholesterol, and exercise. I identified with the comedian Bill Cosby's observation that people in health food stores always look thin, pale, and sad. They might live forever, but they look miserable. In contrast, he noticed that people at a steak house looked healthy, robust, and seemed to be having a great time. They might die the next minute, but they enjoy life.

But, as I got older, I noticed a correlation between my eating and exercise habits and my mental and spiritual well-being. I often drank six cups of coffee and was on edge by noon. To prove caf-

---

1. Michael Quoist quoted in Jerry Bridges, *The Pursuit of Holiness* (Colorado Springs: NavPress, 1978), 111.

feine wasn't to blame, I would lay off for a couple of days. The headaches that followed were hard to discount. Nevertheless, I refused to change.

Until it happened: my blood pressure went up. I did not want to admit it—especially at age 36. My family had a history of high blood pressure, but I was still young.

I talked to my doctor and asked what I could do to bring the pressure down. He questioned my caffeine intake and gave his instructions.

First, he told me to reduce the amount of caffeine in my diet. But I was a caffeine-aholic. Total withdrawal was my only option.

Next, he emphasized the importance of regular exercise. My high blood pressure was a response to inner stress, and my body needed help relaxing. I started taking time out for swimming, walking, and even sit-ups.

Finally, he recommended I drop a few pounds. I was carrying about fifteen pounds more than I should, so I went on a diet. The diet helped me control the amount of sugar I ate and limited between-meal snacks. I cut out ice cream and cookies, and even went cold turkey from donuts.

Now bear in mind, I did this for physiological reasons. I had no serious convictions about body and spirit; I simply wanted to lower my blood pressure.

But I started to see a correlation. I felt better. I woke more invigorated. My spiritual alertness increased. I was starting to say no to my physical hunger—a fruit of the Spirit the Bible calls "self-control." It marks the contrast of a life given to "walking in the flesh." (See Galatians 5:16–25.)

After observing my progress several months, I concluded that physical and spiritual are inter-twined. I summarize it with this simple formula:

GOOD HEALTH
(including regular exercise)

+ GOOD EATING HABITS

= DECREASED STRESS

Doris Janzen Longacre discusses this concept in her *More with Less* cookbook. She contends that North Americans overspend on food and eat too many calories, proteins, sugars, and processed foods. "We are trained to look for convenience and variety, not for nutrition. We are taken in by advertising and by alluring packaging."

Her book encourages a return to simpler eating with more fruit and vegetables, more grains, and what she calls "real food." There is a way of wasting less, eating less, and spending less which gives not less, but more.[2]

The "more" is nutrition, healthy food, and increased mental and spiritual vitality.

So you've heard this all before? All I can tell you is that if you are serious about simplifying your life and decreasing your stress, try it!

Want an apple?

---

2. Doris Janzen Longacre, *The More with Less Cook-book* (New York: Bantam Books, 1981), 12.

WAYS TO SIMPLIFY YOUR LIFE

23. Watch your portions

24. Buy generic

25. Beware of the binge

26. Eat slowly

27. Share recipes and good ideas for health and economical meals

28. Exercise smart. start small and be sensible

29. Grow something

30. Know your limits

31. Just say NO!

32. Take a hike

33. Schedule exercise time

34. Avoid potluck suppers

35. Go fast

36. Exercise with someone

37. Desert desserts

38. Be creative

39. Take the rice and beans challenge

40. Be efficient

41. Consider five points before going to a restaurant

42. Exercise consistently

23

WATCH YOUR PORTIONS

Don't take more food than you will eat. Favor restaurants that serve reasonable rather than "all you can eat" portions. Restaurants serving larger portions encourage us to overeat to "get the most for our money." Taking food home in a "doggie bag" is another alternative to overeating.

24

BUY GENERIC

"Name" brands are often more expensive because we think we're purchasing a better product. By comparing ingredients on the package, we can tell if the extra cost is valid.

25

BEWARE OF THE BINGE

Eat moderately but regularly. Skipping meals often results in eating too much, too fast, and the wrong foods. Gluttony is sin—the lust of the flesh fulfilled!

For business travelers, the boredom of long flights or evenings at motels with nothing to do but eat leads to overeating, leaving us lethargic and upset with ourselves. So, I prepare myself mentally before I travel. I determine to:

- Not eat food "just because it's there."

- Read a book rather than eat another snack.

- Avoid room service even if it is covered by my expense account.

- Exercise regularly to maintain physical control.

26

EAT SLOWLY

You'll feel full sooner. One thing that helped me was to put my fork down between bites. That contrasted my usual "steam shovel" approach of filling the hole with as much as possible as fast as possible.

27

SHARE RECIPES AND GOOD IDEAS FOR HEALTH AND ECONOMICAL MEALS

Consider again the *More with Less* cook book: "Common sense advice and 500 delightful recipes prove that when we reduce our need for heavily grain-fed meat, the super-processed, and the sugary, we not only release resources for the hungry, but also protect our health and our pocket-books."[3]

28

EXERCISE SMART—START SMALL AND BE SENSIBLE

Feeling fat and out-of-shape, I started an exercise program doing 100 sit-ups. I accomplished my goal, but the next day my stomach muscles went into a spasm that gave me hiccups for four days. I finally had to go to the hospital to get a muscle relaxant. A hasty start decreased my desire to exercise.

Last year, I started with ten sit-ups three times per week. Then I added ten per

---

3.   Ibid, back cover.

week with a goal of 100. I learned to start small—the hard way!

29

GROW SOMETHING

It will show suburban and urban children that food is grown; it does not come from the back room of the supermarket or warehouse.

30

KNOW YOUR LIMITS

Stay within a healthy calorie range. Your doctor can prescribe healthy guidelines for you based on age, height, desired weight, and metabolism. Setting limits helps master your appetites rather than your appetites mastering you.

31

JUST SAY NO!

Watch items that are harmful in larger quantities—sugar, caffeine, cholesterol, fats, etc. This might mean cutting back on treats or choosing to drink water rather than soda.

I never realized how much eating sugary desserts at night affected my emotional state in the morning until I went without ice cream for three months. I am sure there is a scientific explanation, but for me it boiled down to sugar at night means a real emotional low the next morning. If I want to wake with vigor, I need to eliminate sugar after 6 p.m.

32

TAKE A HIKE

Walk whenever possible. Take the stairs rather than the elevator.

33

SCHEDULE EXERCISE TIME

Adapt exercise to fit your individual schedule. Mothers with small children may be able to grab an hour of aerobics during nap-time, while an early morning jog might be more practical for a business professional. No single activity works for every lifestyle, so investigate what will work for you.

34

AVOID POTLUCK SUPPERS

Cut back and improve church health by evaluating church functions. Can we offer something healthier?

Starchy casseroles and sugary jello molds are fine for an occasional easy meal. But too often they send the signal that we do not care about what we eat. Many of my missionary friends home on furlough lament the frequent church suppers that inevitably result in gained weight.

Offering fruit rather than donuts, juice rather than sugared beverages, or sal-ads rather than casseroles can start our churches on the road to good health.

35

GO FAST

Consider regular fasting—skipping a meal a week or a day of meals per month. Even partial fasting—cutting certain foods simply to keep appetites under control—can keep us physically and spiritually fit (like Daniel and his friends in Daniel 1:11–16). Many people fast to spend more time in prayer and use the extra money to fight hunger along the lines of Isaiah 58. They fast for a day per week or simply skip a lunch-time meal so that the equivalent amount of money can be given to the relief of hunger and disease for the world's poorest people. Isaiah states that the fast that God chooses serves:

• to loose the chains of injustice
• to untie the cords of the yoke of oppression
• to share your food with the hungry
• to provide the wanderer with shelter
• to clothe the naked (Isaiah 58:6–10)

36

EXERCISE WITH SOMEONE

If I exercise alone watching an aerobic instructor on TV, I am more inclined to be lazy (or even grab a snack while exercising). On the other hand, if Christie and I exercise together, there is accountability and less of a tendency to cheat (see Ecclesiastes 4:9–12).

37

DESERT DESSERTS

We need to change our thinking about desserts. Many of us expect dessert after every main meal rather than as an occasional treat. Cutting out (or at least reducing) desserts can save money, help us lose weight, and diminish our "sugar lows."

38

BE CREATIVE

Address your boredom rather than trying to solve it by eating. This is especially difficult for those who live in colder climates; in the winter when you're feeling cooped up, eating can seem like the only fun available. It takes creativity and a little more preparation, but trips to the library and museum, or a brisk walk stimulate your spirit, mind, and body better than that extra donut!

39

TAKE THE RICE AND BEANS CHALLENGE

Learn to enjoy less expensive staples— like beans, chicken, or rice. You can save money as well as sensitize your family to the fact that many people in the world do not have abundant food options.

40 ———————

BE EFFICIENT

Join a food cooperative. Learn to freeze or can foods. A challenge we occasionally take is to see how many meals we can get out of one turkey. Once the meat is gone, we use the carcass to make turkey soup.

41 ———————

CONSIDER FIVE POINTS BEFORE GOING TO A RESTAURANT

1) Consider take-out food rather than a sit-down restaurant. The main portions

are usually the same size, you avoid the extra calories of rolls and butter, you're less prone to order dessert, and there is no tip.

2) A take-out restaurant lets you dine in the setting of your choice, like a park or by the lake.

3) Is it time to cut back on restaurant eating? Sometimes we eat out because our lives are over-scheduled. Maybe we need to reevaluate our schedules.

4) Don't be duped by image. Gourmet might be synonymous with overpriced. A family restaurant may offer mass-produced, cafeteria-style food.

5) And remember: "fast" food is measured by the speed with which it is produced—not its nutritional value.

42

EXERCISE CONSISTENTLY

It's better to do a little exercise three times a week than a burst of exercise once a month. Twenty minutes of aerobic exercise (where the heart rate is increased) three times per week is ideal. Again, consult your family doctor for advice. Even a small amount of physical activity can awaken your spirit, encourage self-discipline, relieve stress, and give you a healthier outlook.

CHAPTER 4

HOW DO WE SPEND OUR LEISURE TIME?

"I just returned from two weeks' vacation. Why do I feel more exhausted than when I left?" lamented a father who returned to work after taking his family of five on their "dream vacation" to Disney World. "I've used up my vacation time for the year, and our family is worn out. We're tense with each other, and our credit cards are charged to the maximum with the hidden vacation costs."

Sound familiar? Many American consumers have sung the same song of lamentation.

- "The cruise left us bloated and bored."

- "The Caribbean hideaway turned out to be an overpriced shack on a deserted island."

- "The brochure encouraged us to 'live spontaneously,' which turned out to be a euphemism for unbridled credit card spending. Now the bills are rolling in."

OUR CARIBBEAN DISASTER

I know this scenario personally because we have been there. Our trip to the isolated island of Little Cayman (year-round population of under 200) promised to be the vacation of our dreams. We spent more money than we should have, but we rationalized, "We need a rest." We left looking forward to a vacation of isolation and being pampered.

After the six-seater plane touched down on the grass airstrip, our hosts loaded us into the back of the pickup truck owned by our "resort." "Don't worry," I kept telling Christie, "it gets better." (I was confident because the embarrassingly high price we had paid for four nights on Little Cayman could only mean we were headed for a luxury, all-inclusive resort.)

We wanted privacy; we got family-style meals with people who had come to socialize. We hoped to lie on the beach; it was covered with coral and rocks. We were promised a bungalow; we got a screened room so close to the next unit that we could hear our neighbor snore. The brochure promised boat trips; our tiny boat tossed on huge swells while we turned green (I think we kept the Dramamine manufacturers in business that year). And everything cost extra. A Coke was extra. Snorkeling gear was extra. The boat trip was extra. Video rentals were extra. The only thing included in our "all-inclusive" package was our trip back to the airport in the back of the pickup.

Our Little Cayman fiasco illustrated the search thousands of others embark on hoping to find rest, relaxation, and refreshing leisure. And too often we are disappointed. We pursue expensive dreams without contemplating our need for purposeful, restorative leisure.

WHAT ARE WE AFTER?

I heard a story about African missionaries who hired local villagers as porters to help carry supplies to a distant station. The locals went at a slower pace than the missionaries desired, so they pushed them to go faster. On day three of the trek, the group went twice as far as day two. Around the campfire that evening, the missionaries congratulated themselves for their leadership abilities. But on day four, the workers would not budge.

"What's wrong?" asked the missionary.

"We cannot go any further today," replied the villagers' spokesman.

"Why not? Everyone appears well."

"Yes," said the African, "but we went so quickly yesterday that *we must wait here for our souls to catch up with us.*"

It's time to let your soul catch up. We need to put into practice the concept the Bible calls Sabbath—a time when we, like God, rest and get refreshed (Genesis 2:2–8; Exodus 20:8–11). Leisure, in the biblical sense, is a time to slow down and build back our reserves—physically, emotionally, relationally, and spiritually.

Many of us identify with those who are saying, "I want my life back." They abandon the modern pace of life for an escape to the country, a quiet island, or a cabin in the woods. But for most of us, such retreats are mere fantasy—momentary mental escapes from our real world of Blackberrys, mounting mail and email, congested traffic, and over-committed schedules.

Dr. Jeanne Sherrow, formerly professor of Leisure Studies and Resources (our society is so stressed-out that studying leisure is a science!) at the University of Massachusetts, suggests simpler ideas for leisure time in her book *It's About Time*. She invites us all to self-evaluation with these questions:

How long has it been since you . . .

- Took a quiet walk through the woods, pausing long enough on the trail to ponder the wonders about you?

- Sat at water's edge and contemplated its depth, its beauty, its moods?

- Spent the day with your son doing something he especially enjoys and thereby learning new dimensions of him?

- Listened—really listened—to your spouse, or maybe even had an in-depth conversation about something other than work, the house, or the children?

When was the last time you . . .

- Phoned a friend unexpectedly and said, 'Let's go for a walk; it's been a long time since we've had a good chat'?

- Spontaneously organized a group for an evening of games and laughter and fun?

- Read a good book that did something other than entertain you?[1]

Sometimes our pace winds us so tight we can't relax. Driven by our active pace, we choose vacations at "Club Med" or Disney World. Because we can't slow down, we run around on our days off—all the while complaining that our stress is killing us.

Sally McClung suggests four simple exercises to help you unwind:

1) Pause. "Without pausing, our attention stays focused on the situation or problem we are in. We are 'locked' into the tension or pressure of the moment. Pausing can help us break out of the tension."

2) Breathe. Take a deep breath. "Inhale, pause, exhale, pause. . . . Breathing deeply will help us clear the 'cobwebs' out of our brains so that we can think more clearly and resume our work."

---

1.   Jeanne Sherrow, *It's About Time: A Look at Leisure, Lifestyle, and Christianity* (Grand Rapids; Zondervan, 1984), 13–14.

3) Move. "Movement of any kind (stretching, walking around, etc.) actually helps reduce tension."

4) Take a break. "Are your teeth clenched? Neck tight? Shoulders bunched up? Biting your fingernails? Staring off into nowhere? Chewing the inside of your mouth?" These signal that we need a break.[2]

Beyond momentary relaxation, how can you simplify your life so that regular leisure—a time to allow your soul to catch up with you—contributes to your overall well-being? How can you pursue purposeful leisure that glorifies God, renews your family, and remains affordable?

---

2.   Sally McClung, *Where Will I Find the Time?* (Eugene: Harvest House, 1989), 116.

WAYS TO SIMPLIFY
YOUR LIFE

43. Make a memory

44. Enjoy an occasional feast

45. Go for free

46. Play together

47. Consider the lilies and birds

48. Tune-up

49. Get dirty

50. Take a rest with God

51. Exercise for free

52. Plan ahead

53. Commit to loving leisure

54. Cut a firebreak

55. Play for free

56. Look for bargains

57. Witness

58. Strive for balance

59. Listen carefully

60. Rethink Christmas giving

61. Capture opportunities for interpersonal quiet times

62. Dole out the kids

43

MAKE A MEMORY

Instead of using money to buy something, invest in something more meaningful; usually simpler pleasures are less expensive and more refreshing—camping under the stars versus spending the night in a hotel, a walk in the park rather than a trip to the mall, studying the stars instead of going to the movies.

Gloria Gaither and Shirley Dobson co-authored a three-volume set of books for families entitled *Let's Make a Memory*.[3] In these volumes, they offer a myriad of ideas for building family togetherness as children pass through various ages and phases of life.

---

3.   Gloria Gaither and Shirley Dobson, *Let's Make a Memory* (Portland, OR: Multnomah Press, 2005).

44

ENJOY AN OCCASIONAL FEAST

The Bible teaches that "everything God created is good . . . if it is received with thanksgiving" (1 Timothy 4:4–5). There is a time for feasting as well as a time for fasting. Living in freedom means that the vacations we take come as gifts from God, and a dinner at a nice restaurant is our equivalent to biblical "feasting." A simpler lifestyle shouldn't restrict your ability to enjoy life fully and without hesitation. Jesus was accused of partying with sinners and people with bad reputations. His first miracle was making water into wine at a wedding banquet.

Weddings, holidays, anniversaries, birthdays, and other special occasions are times to celebrate life together. An occasional "feast" is certainly endorsed in the Bible through Jesus' example.

The question is, how often? When you simplify your life, be careful to avoid using Scripture to justify your excesses. The key is balance—a simpler life should be enjoyed to its fullest without slipping into a lifestyle of indulgence.

45

GO FOR FREE

Find ways of relaxing for free. Catch up on the latest magazines at the local library or check out a DVD instead of renting one. Read a book rather than shop. Visit a free museum, take a bike ride, go sledding or skating, work on a hobby.

46

PLAY TOGETHER

Learn to relate to each other in a new way. Turn off the TV and bring out the board games. Many people are rediscovering the social benefits (not to mention fun) of games like "Pictionary" or "Uno."

47

CONSIDER THE LILIES AND BIRDS

Develop an appreciation for nature. God "rested and was refreshed" on the Sabbath after he took a long look at His creation.

Take up a "nature" hobby. Our hectic pace separates us from the wonder of God's creation. Growing flowers, observing the industrious and pesky squirrel, or listening to the bird songs can slow us down and help us relax.

We have pursued bird-watching because it is available to us and, after buying binoculars and a basic bird-watching guide, the costs are minimal. The words of John Stott, the great British Bible teacher and author of *The Birds Our Teachers*,[4] influenced us to start. We heard him say, "I've never seen anyone who watches birds suffer from high blood pressure." The relaxation of observing creation refreshes our spirits, our nerves, and our bodies.

48

TUNE-UP

Use music to heighten relaxation. Soothing music on the ride home from work can help us decompress from a tough

---

4. John R. W. Stott, *The Birds Our Teachers: Biblical Lessons from a Lifelong Birdwatcher* (Grand Rapids: Baker Books, 2001.

day. Quiet music can set a tone for thought, prayer, or romance.

I was raised on rock 'n' roll, but I have to admit that while I enjoy listening to rock music, many times in my daily routine the volume and beat were adding to my stress. I noticed that with loud music thumping, I would drive faster. I discovered that Vivaldi's *"Four Seasons"* or some other quiet music serves better than Led Zeppelin to help quiet my soul.

49

GET DIRTY

Working with our hands—in the garden, the yard, or at the workbench—can renew us and change our mental focus. After a particularly difficult day at work, Christie (who works outside the home as a medical technologist) attends her plants. I weed the garden. A half-hour of this type of activity can relieve a headache or relax a tense neck.

For some, "getting dirty" means dusting off an old interest. Michael Foster says, "Leisure is the mother of discovery."[5] So, take up that paintbrush, dust off that camera, or resume writing poetry.

50

TAKE A REST WITH GOD

Meditate on the Psalms, or examine texts like Matthew 11:28–30. It will bring your perspective in line with God's.

We live in a culture that says, "He who dies with the most toys wins." Distinctly biblical concepts like contentment (Philippians 4:11) or freedom from the love of money (1 Timothy 6:6–10) remind us that biblical leisure is a time for refreshing and recreation, renewing and resting our body and soul.

---

5.   Sally McClung, 120.

51

EXERCISE FOR FREE

Try to exercise at minimal cost: walk the stairs, play basketball at the public courts, or swim at a community pool. Luxury gyms and work-out facilities are usually expensive and often tense environments. And if we've paid for the membership fees, we may feel guilty if we do not go use the facility. Why not jog on the street rather than on somebody else's $500 treadmill?

52

PLAN AHEAD

Tour packages are popular because they require no planning on our part. Leisure time is a gift from God that we should plan as we would our work. Our leisure time can be more than just "goofing off." It can be a purposeful change of pace.

This change of pace should include "down time"—a chance to give our minds a rest and stare at the ocean, watch TV, or take a nap. An old poster states, "Sometimes I sits and thinks, and sometimes I just sits." We need both.

53

COMMIT TO LOVING LEISURE

Remember the poor. We budget money each year for a "vacation with purpose"—using vacation time for a short-term mission, or because we have a double-income household, we can set aside money to help someone who might not otherwise be able to afford a vacation.

54

CUT A FIREBREAK

When a forest fire burns uncontrollably, firefighters do not fight the fire directly. They move ahead of the fire's path and cut the trees down so that the fire has nothing to consume. When the fire reaches the firebreak, it burns itself out.

When our schedules burn out of control, we look ahead and plan a day we can stop to regain our sanity. These days off function as firebreaks. Or, to change analogies, they allow us to "come up for air" after we have been submerged too long.

The anticipation of the day off ahead (or the vacation ahead) helps us persevere until a break is possible.

Note: to avoid out-of-control demands on our time, Christie and I schedule our days off three to six months in advance. Even if we cannot honor every one, planning ahead keeps us from going for weeks without a break.

55

PLAY FOR FREE

Choose an inexpensive sport or hobby— basketball or running versus golf or skiing, cross-country skiing versus downhill, etc.

In this spirit, you can also simplify by buying equipment according to real need. A weekend tennis player who spends exorbitantly on a racket may be buying more than he needs. The same is true of athletic shoes. If I play recreational basketball once a week or less, do I need NBA-endorsed athletic shoes that cost $200?

56

LOOK FOR BARGAINS

Airlines, for example, offer discounted rates for those who are willing to book ahead and stay over Saturday night. Websites like Travelocity or Expedia exist specifically to help people find the cheapest possible travel options.

Christie and I once flew to San Francisco from Boston for $99 total (round-trip) using advance purchases, unusual travel routings, and a two-for-one coupon we had clipped from a travel magazine. We were delighted that we had saved money, but we spent two days (out of a seven-day vacation) just getting there and getting home. The experience taught us a valuable lesson: when pursuing leisure options, we need to ask, "Which is more limited—our time or our money?" If the goal is rest, sometimes spending the money might be better than burning up limited time. It goes back to our need for purposely, forward-planning of our leisure.

57

WITNESS

Some people are more open to talking about the meaning of life when they are relaxed. Vacation times or days off can provide opportunities to engage in discussions about what it means to follow Jesus Christ.

58

STRIVE FOR BALANCE

Try to take regular time off so you do not binge on extravagant vacations after months without a day off, like Christie and I did on our Little Cayman fiasco.

59

LISTEN CAREFULLY

Use vacations and days off to listen to God. So often we fill our days with noise and activity. We return from leisure more exhausted than when we left. It always saddens me to watch a jogger on the shoreline at Cape Cod wearing head phones rather than listening to the pounding surf. In a world filled with noise, we need to quiet ourselves to hear God's voice.

60

RETHINK CHRISTMAS GIVING

Christie introduced me to "Advent Promises" shortly after we got married, and it never fails to add meaning to Christmas, even as it decreases our expenses. Rather than gifts, we give each other promises throughout the month of December. She gets the odd days, and I get the even. On my day, I give her a gift certificate promising to do something I do not usually do. She can claim the promise that day or anytime during the month. She might promise to serve me breakfast in bed or take over my vacuuming responsibilities for a week. I might promise to do the laundry for a month or go shopping without complaining.

61

CAPTURE OPPORTUNITIES FOR INTERPERSONAL QUIET TIMES

Refreshment in our closest relationships comes from the ability to converse. In worlds filled with noise, iPods, and chatter, our dialogue is often only sharing news.

To keep sanity in our daily lives, Christie and I have adopted the British custom of teatime around 4 PM—sort of a daily mini-inter-personal Sabbath. We take a break in the day to talk—no music, reading the mail, or answering phone calls. For about twenty to thirty minutes, we talk. We discuss the day's events, listen to each other, and prepare for the evening.

Teatime might not fit every couple's schedule, but some version of what someone called "marital quiet time," allows our souls to catch up with each other as well as ourselves.

62

DOLE OUT THE KIDS

Leisure is often a luxury for parents, especially parents of young children. Many parents are bartering with other parents for child care.

By joining together with others who can swap baby-sitting responsibilities, couples are able to have an occasional evening or day alone. It may only be one day in three weeks, but one day is better than no days.

CHAPTER 5

TO THE BEAT OF A DIFFERENT DRUMMER

The way we celebrated Christmas illustrated our divergent views. Christie and I exchanged a few stocking stuffers—favorite candy or other little gifts, and one significant gift. I think I gave her earrings; she gave me a beautiful sweater.

Not so our friends Jack and Fran, a childless couple like us with whom we were celebrating. We went over to their home about noon. They were still opening gifts. The couch and the floor in front of it were covered with brightly colored packages. A new coat, several pieces of jewelry, CDs, sweaters, skirts, and blouses for her. For him, Brooks

Brothers shirts, a cashmere overcoat, more sweaters, a suit, electronic gadgets, and a host of other items. We watched as the loot increased and they "oohed" and "ahhed" at every new discovery. We could not estimate the cumulative total of what they spent on each other, but we knew it was in the thousands of dollars.

After the bundle extravaganza ended, they asked, "So what did you give each other?" We felt small and cheap. We wanted to lie or exaggerate our gifts lest they think we were having marital problems. We told them about our one gift to each other. They felt embarrassed and guilty as they looked over their treasure chest. We wondered if they were going to take up an offering for us.

Our contrasting approach to Christmas celebration left us feeling very uneasy. Simplifying our lives will do that. We begin to feel like we took a detour from the mainstream of society, and we no longer "fit."

Cutting back can leave us feeling like what the Bible calls "aliens and strangers" in the world. It is Christian living amidst the values of a non-Christian society (or even a Christian culture absorbed by the values of our materialistic world)

THE EMPEROR IS NAKED

Remember the fable *"The Emperor's New Clothes"*? The clever tailors appeal to the emperor's vanity, convincing him that only the wisest and most discriminating people will be able to see the robe they will create for him. He commissions them to do it, and so they go to work weaving imaginary thread into cloth. The emperor cannot see it, but he will not admit it.

The wealthiest people of the city are told the same thing: only the most sophisticated will be able to see this robe. When the day of the unveiling arrives, the emperor struts out to show this masterful creation. He is stark naked, but no one will admit it because to do so would imply poor taste in clothes or low social status.

But a little boy speaks up: "The emperor is naked." Others begin to speak up as well. The emperor had been conned by the tailors and misled by his ego.

The little boy illustrates the role that Christians fill in a world conned by the Deceiver, misled by pride, and duped by false advertising. We are the ones who announce that:

- Living to acquire possessions that offer no hope or lasting fulfillment is naked.

- Measuring your worth or love for others with financial price tags is naked.

- Sacrificing relationships in search of career success is naked.

- Materialism (the ethical doctrine that material self-interest should determine conduct) is naked.

- Living without eternal perspective is naked.

God's people should be the ones identifying the cultural values of our day as "naked."

A TV commercial a few years ago featured the tennis star Andre Agassi. It was at a stage in his life when his reputation was that of a fast-paced playboy living a "glitzy" lifestyle of fast cars, luxury travel, beautiful people and exorbitant wealth. The commercial flashed through his lifestyle, and then he delivered his pitch for the camera, reminding us that "image is everything."

Image drives people to purchase homes that are too large, lease SUV's which get terrible gas mileage, and maximize their credit cards to present an image of being wealthier than they are. The advertising world tries to convince us that we can purchase image, but it's a horrible expensive, spiritually shallow way to live.

When we—like the emperor—start believing "image is everything," we will find ourselves pursuing values that contradict God's values. In contrast, simplifying our lives implies we march to the beat of God's drum in contrast to Madison Avenue's.

WAYS TO SIMPLIFY
YOUR LIFE

63. Evaluate

64. Tell the truth

65. Be moderate

66. Just say no!

67. Investigate

68. Consider a "plastectomy"

69. Stop and smell the roses

70. Be a trustee

71. Evaluate your commitment to sports

72. Open doors

73. Minimize hypocrisy

74. Ask why—related to moral choices

75. Offer support

76. Be humble

77. Untwist the wording

78. Stay away from the "Stuff-Mart"

79. Look beneath the surface

80. Read the fine prinT

81. Don't bow down to technology

82. Focus on the real needs of your family

83. Rediscover the holidays

84. Take the Micah 6:8 test

85. Don't be squeezed

63

EVALUATE

To what extent do you need to be "up with the latest fashions"? Following Jesus may mean you feel a little out of date at times. Remember the term "planned obsolescence"? It means that marketers intentionally design things to go out of style. If three-piece suits are in style, marketers are creating plans to promote double-breasted blazers.

Whether skirt length, wide ties versus narrow, or carpet color, advertising creates a hunger for something. But after a short period, any material purchase will leave you dissatisfied again.

Thinking counter-culturally frees you from being a slave to clever marketing.

64

TELL THE TRUTH

In an interview entitled, "Debt Man Talking," financial advisor Dave Ramsey made the disturbing observation that marriages are getting into trouble because spouses are lying to each other about their credit card spending. He estimated that 37 percent of couples had "a hidden debt or a hidden bank account or a hidden agenda with money that he or she didn't want the other spouse to know about."[1]

Obviously such hiding is not only a recipe for financial woes, but it also plants the seeds of deceit in the relationship. Tell each other the truth and manage your finances together.

---

1.   John Carroll, "Debt Man Talking," *American Way Magazine* (December 1, 2006), 32–33.

65

BE MODERATE

Simplifying your life means trying to be culturally relevant but not excessive. The intent is to blend in so we are neither extravagant nor dowdy. And this applies to far more than clothing. It could apply to choice of vacation, home, or where to take clients for a business lunch.

Michelle needed a college education. At nineteen, her goal was to get a bachelor's degree and then go to graduate school. She took a lot of pressure off her family and herself when she transferred from a private university to a state school—a decision that saved her and her family tens of thousands of dollars.

Did she get "the best education money could buy"? Probably not. Were her mental capacities fully developed? Who knows? But Michelle concluded that a private university would not offer an education that is three or four times better, especially since it would put her more than $30,000 in debt by the time she started graduate school.

Michelle thought counter-culturally, enabling her to withstand the criticism that she was "wasting her potential" at a state school. And she went on to graduate with her Master's degree from the program and university of her choice.

66 ——————

JUST SAY NO!

If your job threatens your health, your family, or your relationship with God, it is time to look for a new job.

67

INVESTIGATE

Ask questions our materialistic culture never will to steer clear of what Tony Campolo calls "conspicuous consumption." Our society may actually endorse materialistic decisions opposed to following Christ. For instance:

- Is a second car justified?

- If so, do you need a 4-wheel-drive SUV if you never drive off-road?

- Is a vacation home really needed?

- If you get a vacation home, have you calculated the financial and time expenditure needed in the upkeep and servicing of that home?

- Should you rent or buy a home? It's more than an issue of equity or taxes; there is the question of being unable to act if God calls you elsewhere.

- Is "keeping up with the Joneses" a biblical value?

68

CONSIDER A "PLASTECTOMY"

Credit card debt getting you down? How about a "plastectomy"—radical surgery involving the removal and destruction of all credit cards? Financial advisors insist it may be the only way that some can cure obsessive buying habits.

Perhaps a milder alternative for most might be trying to go three months without using credit cards. I know it might complicate life on one hand because of issues of cash flow and larger purchases, but could you do it?

Some object, "But what about the 'frequent-user' award programs?"—those awards of air-miles or dozens of other incentives to spend? Remember how advertisers spin the words to get you to buy? Well, those "awards" are not awards; they're incentives to get us into more purchasing and greater debt. And you don't "earn" them as if you're working for them; you're buying them.

69

STOP AND SMELL THE ROSES

You can enjoy beauty in the world—art, music, creation, etc.—without making it your God. Simplifying your life means enjoyment without obsession. If your dedication to art, photography, or music grows stronger than your devotion to Jesus, you become an idolater.

70

BE A TRUSTEE

The Bible teaches us to be stewards of possessions, money, resources, and even of the "mysteries of God." Seeing ourselves in this light reminds us that we are trustees of someone else's estate.

Stewardship, however, is no excuse for laziness or irresponsibility toward money or possessions. Scripture exhorts us to be wise in the resources with which we have been entrusted.

71

EVALUATE YOUR COMMITMENT TO SPORTS

Sports—whether we participate or spectate—can be great sources of joy and relaxation. But an over-attachment to sports can help spin our lives out of control. Nothing illustrates this more than the fact that athletes in the United States receive millions of dollars each year because we pay to watch them shoot, pitch, hit, or throw.

I confronted my own imbalance with sports several years ago. As a native Bostonian, I had been raised on Celtics basketball. I loved to watch them play, and they rewarded me with multiple championships. When I was younger, meeting Bob Cousy or Larry Bird would be like meeting one of the apostles.

But as the team's prowess waned and the championships came less often, I found myself getting angry with the team. If they lost, I felt emotionally let down. My well-being was controlled by their win/loss column—as if the basketball season had any real significance in history!

Finally, I snapped out of it. Spectator sports are entertainment. The athletes are playing a *game*. If the outcome of the season determines my emotional or spiritual health, I am absorbed by values the world says are acceptable but which do not fit God's kingdom priorities.

72

OPEN DOORS

Many non-Christians prefer the moral climate Christians create. Living counter-culturally can attract people to Jesus.

In my youth ministry experience, I found that many parents who did not attend church encouraged their teens to participate in youth groups where sexual promiscuity is discouraged. Many non-believers enjoy and often prefer alcohol-free parties. People who hunger for relationships are drawn to biblical values of marriage and family taught in the church.

Marching to the beat of God's drum draws people to the truth of the Gospel.

73

MINIMIZE HYPOCRISY

Ask yourself, "Will this action/purchase/decision help me live with greater integrity so that my words and my actions mesh?"

Living the Christian life in a materialistic culture where everyone is stressed and overburdened presents a tremendous challenge. Our goal is to grow so that our convictions are applied to our own lives. "Minimizing hypocrisy" means developing our character along with our convictions.

We might promote our churches as a place to meet Jesus and find "rest for your soul," but the hectic church schedules contradict what we say. Sundays become just another day of stress rather than rest.

"Minimizing hypocrisy" in this case means that church leaders question how to revise the program so that people find rest for their souls.

74

ASK WHY— RELATED TO MORAL CHOICES

When we venture into the world as Jesus did, we need to question whether our motives and intentions are to increase our effectiveness as "salt" and "light" in the world, or simply to satisfy our sinful lusts.

So, in the spirit of marching to God's drum, ask these questions:

- Why am I going to this "R" rated movie? Is it to understand something about the world I am trying to evangelize or to satisfy my voyeuristic and lustful curiosity?

- Why do I take a liberal view of alcohol? Is it to gain admission into the world of social drinkers so that I can reach them or merely to get away with drinking?

- Why am I careless with my language? Will people be more responsive to me if I cuss or am I just being naughty?

75

OFFER SUPPORT

Simpler living does not mean retreating to a Christian commune or monastery. As God's people, we need to support aspects of the culture that promote biblical values (even if they are not directly initiated by Christians) such as justice, fairness, morality, and care for the poor. The idea of living more simply so that others may simply live is not exclusively Christian.

76 —————

BE HUMBLE

Go out of your way to meet and interact with the poor and needy, imitating Jesus who, "though he was rich, yet for [our] sakes he became poor" (2 Corinthians 8:9).

The desire to keep economic pace with our neighbors often keeps us from simplifying our lives. This value, however, does not give us much time to compare ourselves against those who have far less than we do.

A high school student, after visiting a barrio in Colombia remarked, "In the Third World, they do not hide their poor people as well as we do."

Humility—derived from the word humus, which means to keep close to the soil—calls us to bring the poor out of "hiding" so we will learn simplicity and contentment.

St. Francis de Sales presented this message in his book, *Introduction to the Devout Life*: "If you love the poor, be often with them. Be glad to see them in your own home and to visit with them in theirs. Be glad to talk to them and be pleased to have them near you in church, on the street, and elsewhere."[2]

77

UNTWIST THE WORDING

Don't be fooled by semantics. By changing from "sneakers" to "athletic footwear,"

---

2. Francis de Sales, *Introduction to the Devout Life*, quoted in *Discipleship Journal*, (Issue 25, 1985):

merchandisers increase the price because we conclude that we are getting more for our money. So remember, the word for sunglasses is "protective eyewear," macaroni and cheese is now "pasta formaggio," and hamburger is "chopped steak."

78

STAY AWAY FROM THE "STUFF-MART"

In a humorous episode of "Veggie Tales," the wealthy Madame Blueberry tries to satisfy her pursuit of happiness by going to the "Stuff-Mart" to buy every product she ever dreamed of. Basket after basket of stuff roles out the door to her home (later in the episode her tree house gets overloaded and eventually destroyed by all of the stuff). But in the meantime, Madame Blueberry has discovered that stuff cannot make her happy. "A happy heart" is not for sale at the Stuff-Mart.

Charles Colson identifies our culture with Madame Blueberry's pursuits: "Paradoxically, striving for possessions and money, the things we think will bring us pleasure and happiness, actually strips the meaning from our lives. We become cynical and crass. Life becomes banal."[3]

We all need to internalize the lesson of this children's show because shopping at the equivalent of the Stuff-Mart has become a culturally-acceptable solution for dealing with unhappiness—remember the bumper sticker that read "When the going gets tough, the tough go shopping!"

Remember Madame Blueberry's lesson: a happy heart is not for sale at the Stuff-Mart, in the Mall, on the home shopping network, in the catalog, or through the Internet.

---

3.   Charles Colson with Harold Fickett, *The Good Life: Seeking Purpose, Meaning, and Truth in Your Life* (Wheaton: Tyndale House Publishers, 2005), 51.

79

LOOK BENEATH
THE SURFACE

A couple Christie and I befriended several years ago chartered a yacht (including the skipper and crew) for a two-week vacation. We knew that their income was roughly the same as ours, but we also knew that we could not afford the thousands of dollars they spent on such a vacation for ourselves. The difference? We give away over 10 percent of our income; they don't.

If we follow the Christian mandate to be generous and the biblical teaching on tithing (giving at least 10 percent), we will find ourselves falling behind the lifestyle of noncontributing peers.

80

READ THE FINE PRINT

Read that "special restrictions apply" paragraph on the vacation package or the small print on the warranty. We can often discover half-truths which deceive us into buying impulsively. Before purchasing a new car, remember to factor in the extra costs of excise tax and increased insurance payments.

81

DON'T BOW DOWN TO TECHNOLOGY

Technological advances increase with such rapidity that they can leave all of us worrying that the world is marching on while we get further and further behind.

We try to address this fear by increasing our technological support lest we fall back into the Dark Ages.

So we buy faster and better computers, add more features to our phone service, and purchase the latest in electronic gadgetry. We want homes "wired" for the Internet, cell-phones that give us the capacity to be available 24–7, and home entertainment systems with higher resolution and more vivid colors, while occupying less and less space. And even then, after have spent thousands trying to stay current, we read about some new, smaller MP3 player and we wonder how long we can manage without it.

Technological advances can offer great support to the busy person, but sometimes we need to step back and evaluate whether it will increase our effectiveness and decrease our stress. Or will it be just the opposite? Every new advance in technology demands time to learn, set-up, maintain, and respond to.

Technology is our servant. Switch off the phone for a quiet night at home. Answering voice mail or email messages can wait. If the family budget is strained because you buy DVD's to justify owning the plasma TV, stop and reconsider! Don't let technology become your master.

82

FOCUS ON THE REAL NEEDS OF YOUR FAMILY

Christian parents often struggle over what constitutes proper care of their family. Like a pendulum, they can swing between two extremes—neglecting responsibilities at home to focus exclusively on following Jesus, or deifying the family.

Parents become anxious to provide the perfect growth environment for their children, all the while fearing they will make a tragic mistake that will scar their emotional or spiritual well-being.

While every parent desires healthy children, it's important to maintain some balance. Children remind us that we are out of control. Striving for a perfect family can bump Jesus from the center of our lives. The family then becomes an idol.

83

REDISCOVER THE HOLIDAYS

Living more simply frees us from some of the materialism of the holidays—especially Christmas and birthdays. The countercultural viewpoint keeps us from blocking out Jesus from Christmas with tinsel and packages. Birthdays can become a celebration of someone's life rather than merely an exercise in gift-giving.

84

TAKE THE MICAH 6:8 TEST

God's priorities for us are summarized in Micah 6:8. What does God want from us? To act justly, love mercy, and walk humbly with God.

On a day-to-day level, we can evaluate how well we are marching to the beat of God's drum by asking questions like:

- Am I acting justly? Do I care about fairness? Do the companies that produce the products I purchase promote a just environment for their workers?

- Do I love mercy? Am I caring for people in need? Does mercy characterize the way I interact with others?

- Am I walking humbly with God? Am I striving to understand His agenda for my life or simply seeking His seal of approval on my own agenda?

85

DON'T BE SQUEEZED

The J.B. Phillips translation of Romans 12:2 reads, "Don't let the world squeeze you into its mold." That is a great summary of the countercultural challenge. Ask yourself if the world is influencing your values, attitudes, or behaviors in the following areas:

- Relationships—in the home, the church, or the community.

- Possessions—want versus need.

- Values or dreams—our priorities, our personal "mission statement."

Remember, "Lives based on having are less free than lives based either on doing or on being."[4]

---

4.   William James, quoted in John Gardner *Self Renewal* (New York: Harper and Row, 1964), 63.

CHAPTER 6

OUR LIVES AND OUR TIME

In a letter from a war-torn country in Africa, one Christian leader wrote, "The greatest need in our country is for God's people to *act* Christian." His concern was not for orthodox belief or theological purity. The cognitive state of the Christians in his country remained sound. His concern was lifestyle: living out the Christian faith in daily practice.

To act Christian. What does it mean? Evangelism? Bible study? Prayer? Certainly all of these disciplines play a part, but there is more. To live a Christian lifestyle means that our faith affects every area of our lives—the chicken pot pie outlook versus the TV dinner. Remember?

How do we relate to material things? Is an ascetic life of voluntary poverty the Christian norm? Does acting Christian affect how we plan our schedules? What does it mean to act Christian in cultures of affluence?

IN PURSUIT OF SIMPLER LIVING

Jeff and Judy Heath, members of our church who eventually went on to serve with Wycliffe Bible Translators in Africa, were teaching the young couples class about living more simply. They defined simpler living to their Sunday School class this way:

> To live a simple lifestyle means to live intentionally beneath your potential standard of living for the purpose of sharing your excess with others. "Lifestyle" includes housing, clothes, transportation, food, use of time, and future plans.

The question of a simplified life comes up for a variety of reasons:

- It might be that our pace was killing us and we wanted to cut back.

- We may grow aware through the news or through a short-term mission trip that there are millions of people living in countries in Africa, Asia, and Latin America (or in our own urban centers in our own country) who are extremely poor, and this knowledge may have convicted us of wastefulness.

• Our abundance may be dulling our spirits, and we have decided to return to a biblical detachment from possessions.

The Heaths, who intentionally simplified their lifestyle long before they left to serve in Africa, cite the following benefits of living more simply:

• Benefits to us personally:

   o Helps us focus on more important things.

   o Decreases our stress.

   o Improves our physical health.

   o Helps us break away from compulsive buying habits.

• Benefits to our relationship with God:

   o Allows more time for Him.

   o Heightens our dependence on Him.

o   Teaches us to receive our self-worth from Him rather than our possessions or accomplishments.

o   Keeps us from becoming self-sufficient and forgetting God (see Proverbs 30:7–9).

o   Honors God by honoring the poor (see Deuteronomy 15:7–8, 10–11).

- Benefits for others:

o   Frees up time and energy for relationships.

o   Frees up funds to give to those in need.

o   Closes the gap between rich and poor allowing us to become equals in Christ.

Whatever the reason, a simpler life is a worthwhile pursuit. The payoff is improved health, spiritual well-being, and a better world. It frees up time for personal growth as we learn to resist the self-destructive tendencies of workaholism, consumerism, and materialism.

TRAVELING LIGHT

The Christian journey improves when we make intentional choices to lighten our load. To use the backpacker's analogy again, the simpler lifestyle enables us to dump the unnecessary stuff that weighs us down.

Tom Sine offers this challenge:

First-century Christians understood that following Jesus was a whole-life commitment. They committed everything to Christ. Today we're taught we can have everything we want, including lavish homes and expensive cars, as long as we have a right attitude, as long as we aren't materialistic. Today we can be a spiritual leader in the church and never leave the church building. Seventy-five percent of the people I meet in churches have no time to minister to anyone else.

But God has entrusted us with only a certain amount of money, time, and education. The more of those resources I spend on my own life and local church, the less is available to advance God's kingdom.[1]

---

1. Tom Sine, "Will the Real Cultural Christians Please Stand Up?" *World Vision* (October-November 1989), 22. Reprinted by permission of World Vision Magazine, Used by permission.

Russ Reinert, formerly a personnel director for a mission agency working in Peru, indicated that overloaded "packs" beset even those in cross-cultural work: "When I went to the mission field in 1969, we left everything to follow Jesus. Today's missionaries take everything with them. I brought two suitcases and one barrel; they bring two containers, the equivalent size of a trailer truck, full of stuff—much of which will separate them from the people they're trying to serve."

Traveling light presents a radical approach to living as God's people, but that's what a simpler lifestyle is all about.

WAYS TO SIMPLIFY YOUR LIFE

86. Give purposefully

87. Give strategically

88. Look outward

89. Prevent "consumptivitis"

90. Choose housing wisely

91. Reduce your housing debt

92. Don't pursue the largest mortgage a bank will approve

93. Give it away

94. Question your purchases

95. Ask why. related to use of time and money

96. Be reasonable

97. Form a cooperative

98. Give to God what is God's

99. Make the best use of your time

86

GIVE
PURPOSEFULLY

With solicitations coming through the mail, over the phone, and even through our churches, we need to plan our giving to maximize its impact. Putting a few dollars into a myriad of projects fragments its effect.

Better to choose a few areas—the homeless, hunger, AIDS research, or outreach to children—and invest heavily rather than give $10 to numerous organizations.

Purposeful giving demands solutions. The proverb states, "Give a man a fish and you feed him for a day; teach a man to fish and you feed him for a lifetime." We give to promote effective farming techniques, not simply food relief. Others invest in job retraining programs that offer a fresh start to the homeless and unemployed.

87

GIVE STRATEGICALLY

Look for ministries that do the most with your money. A variety of resources exist to help Christian givers discern the best and most efficient organizations. Generally speaking, a ministry that spends more than 20 percent of its budget on overhead needs to be evaluated.[2]

Many churches try to balance strategic giving with concrete ways to be involved. World Vision's "30-hour Fast,"[3] opportunities in Short-Term Missions, and seasonal events like the "Angel Tree"[4] all can serve this purpose.

Many ministries promote small-but-strategic giving opportunities through

2.   Find information at the web site of the Evangelical Council for Financial Accountability: www.ecfa.org.

3.   Find information at www.worldvision.org.

4.   Find information on The Angel Tree or Christmas Shoebox at www.samaritanspurse.org.

"alternative gift-giving" ideas. People donate a sum of money as a gift in the name of a friend which will purchase anything from seeds to sewing machines for poor families, World Relief,[5] World Vision,[6] Samaritan's Purse[7] and many others offer these opportunities. In my name, a friend gave a donkey and cart to a farmer in the Philippines. Women in our church bought two hogs for a Latin American farmer. We gave part of a community health training program in Mozambique in the names of two of our friends.

Strategic giving asks, "Where will my gift have long-lasting impact for those in need?"

5.   www.worldrelief.org or www.wr.org

6.   www.worldvision.org

7.   www.samaritanspurse.org

88

LOOK OUTWARD

Make time for others. The essence of the Christian life is serving without reciprocation (see 1 John 3:17–18). If all of our time is spent on friends at church, we need to reevaluate. The church is supposed to benefit non-members, yet much of our time is spent socializing and we don't meet people outside the church.

Simplifying here might mean cutting a few church programs to serve those outside the kingdom of God, like Tom did. He quit the church softball team to join a league in the community where he would meet non-Christians. Sadly, his greatest opposition came from church members!

Simplifying might also mean looking for opportunities to serve outside our socio-economic strata. One businessman leaves the financial district of Boston (where he works) at lunchtime once a week to serve meals at an inner city soup kitchen, "It reminds me that my world is not the 'norm' for many people." Reaching out to those less fortunate will also make us grateful for what we have.

89

PREVENT "CONSUMPTIVITIS"

A simpler lifestyle means living at a prescribed limit rather than expanding our lifestyle when our income increases. This might not be relevant in hard economic times, but it is a sound financial discipline in times of prosperity. Charles Colson observes how our culture has changed:

In one generation, America has experienced a dramatic transformation from a producing society to a consuming society . . . (Instead of measuring by output, we now measure our economy based on consumption.) We have completely reversed the Protestant work ethic. . . . At the heart of the work ethic was a belief that one should work hard, be thrifty, save, and produce. Delayed gratification was a virtue. Today the concept of delayed gratification is seen as a denial of some inherent natural right.[8] (parenthetical comment mine)

Limiting ourselves means we determine what we need to live and stay within those limits. Adjust for inflation or increased family size, but avoid "consumptivitis" which spends according to income and desire rather than according to predetermined need and discipline.

8. Charles Colson with Harold Fickett, *The Good Life: Seeking Purpose, Meaning, and Truth in Your Life* (Wheaton: Tyndale House Publishers, 2005), 46.

90

CHOOSE HOUSING WISELY

Before buying a home, decide which neighborhood will foster your sense of appreciation and contentment or (in contrast) your sense of covetousness or envy.

Realistically, contentment is subjective. Living in a small house in an affluent neighborhood might cause more dissatisfaction because you will always feel like you are the paupers in the land of wealth. Better to choose an average home in an average neighborhood if it enhances your sense of contentment.

91

REDUCE YOUR HOUSING DEBT

We decided as soon as we signed our mortgage to pay it off as quickly as possible to save thousands of dollars in interest. We repaid a loan a few years ago that was costing us $350 per month. Instead of looking at this as a new source of spending money (after all, we had been living without it up to that point), we started paying an extra $350 per month on the principal of our mortgage. We estimate that a faster pay-off of our mortgage will save over $100,000 in interest payments. (Note: I am not a financial analyst and opinions may vary on mortgage repayments and interest deductions on taxes, but I believe that getting out of debt as quickly as possible is biblically sound even if our financial counselor disagrees.)

92

DON'T PURSUE THE LARGEST MORTGAGE A BANK WILL APPROVE

Remember . . . lenders depend on your indebtedness. The more you owe, the more interest they receive. Much prosperity in the past has come from increased indebtedness not increased productivity. Writing in March 2007, Michael Hodges states that America's total debt has surpassed $48 trillion (which includes government debt). He elaborates: "$48 trillion—that's $161,287 per man, woman and child—or $645,148 per family of four, $45,514 more debt per family than last year."[9] Like the bumper sticker says, we have been living off our children's inheritance.

One of the greatest questions facing young families and working professionals

---

9. http://mwhodges.home.att.net/nat-debt/debt-nat.htm.

is whether or not to buy a home. Study the market. In a down economy, or an inflated housing market, it may be wiser to rent and wait for the optimum combination of price, mortgage rate, and location.

93

GIVE IT AWAY

"Of the accumulation of things there is no end" paraphrases one of the messages of the Book of Ecclesiastes. A simpler lifestyle chooses to unclutter and avoids saving things because "they might be useful someday."

For us, this means regular give-aways to a homeless shelter in Boston or to the Salvation Army. Another "give away" idea: we tag our clothes hangers once a year and remove the tag when the clothes are worn. If a tag is still there after a year, we know that shirt, skirt, or pair of pants should be given to someone who can use it.

94

QUESTION YOUR PURCHASES

Before making a major purchase, ask yourself, "How could this money be used to bring greater glory to Christ?" It is a tough question because it makes you reconsider an otherwise legitimate purchase, but it confirms your priority to first follow Christ.

95

ASK WHY— RELATED TO USE OF TIME AND MONEY

Someone said, "Satan does not steal our answers; he steals our questions." We often forget to ask "Why?" Simpler living asks why. Why do I need this product? Why should I believe the promises of a brochure? Why must I attend events that may or may not have significant purpose? Why respond to an opportunity just because it's there?

96

BE REASONABLE

A pressure for middle-aged adults is planning for retirement. We consult with insurers and financial counselors, and they urge us to be prepared for every contingency.

With respect to retirement, we need to ask, "How can we plan ahead and still live by faith?" Christians should save for a "reasonable" retirement remembering that God directs us to trust our future to Him.

97

FORM A COOPERATIVE

Do we need to own everything? We can save hundreds of dollars by co-owning lawn mowers, washers and dryers, and kitchen appliances we use only sporadically. We can simplify while enhancing "neighborliness" by sharing, swapping, and being creative.

98

GIVE TO GOD WHAT IS GOD'S

Look at your use of time, your expenditures, and your real priorities (the ones you live by rather than the ones you claim to live by). Ask, "Am I living with eternal values in mind, believing that God and people are the only things that will last?" Tom Sine writes,

> What we see in the New Testament is whole-life stewardship. If we accept the premise that the earth is the Lord's, then it's no longer how much of mine I must relinquish; the question becomes how much of God's do I get to keep in a world where many Christians can't even keep their kids fed. . . . The popular myth is that if we give God 10 percent, then what we do with the rest is our own business. Such a view simply isn't biblical. The earth is the Lord's; so is everything that we own.[10]

10. Tom Sine, "Shifting Stewardship into the Future Tense," *NAE Action* (March/April, 1990), 9.

99

MAKE THE BEST
USE OF YOUR TIME

Make multiple use of your time. Ask yourself, "How else can I use this time?" You might bring necessary reading to the doctor or dentist office while you wait rather than thumb through magazines. You might do laundry with a friend, listen to tapes while driving, or catch up on correspondence while away on a business trip.

100

DO THE HARDEST
TASKS FIRST

Put those dreaded tasks at the top of your "to do" list and take care of them first. Procrastinating only makes them

seem harder and can keep them on your
list for weeks.

Whether it is paying the bills, going
to the dentist, or calling Aunt Mabel, do
yourself a favor by tackling the tough as-
signments first.

101

HANDLE TASKS IN "CLUMPS"

Rather than paying bills as they arrive,
set aside an entire evening each week or
two for bookkeeping. Set aside another
evening for catching up on emails and
other correspondence. Buy birthday cards
three to six months in advance and file
them according to the date they need to
be mailed.

For larger families, freezers or food
storage closets make sense. If you live far
from a market you can buy at a wholesale
store; buying food in quantities can save

you time and money. A food cooperative may also be a good idea.

102

SAVE TIME AND ENERGY BY UNDERSTANDING YOUR INDIVIDUAL CLOCK

A morning person may get more done between 7 a.m. and 11 a.m. than any other time of the day. A night person may never see 7 a.m.; he or she may get up to speed two hours after I have gone to sleep.

Working according to my individual clock teaches me how to approach my tasks. If I'm a morning person, I need to block out the early hours of each day for study, planning, and thinking. Administrative tasks can wait until after noon.

Understanding others' schedules can help us save time as well. For instance, we can shop when stores are less busy, make medical appointments before the doctor has a chance to get behind, and plan personal quiet time when the children are quiet.

103

SCHEDULE A FAMILY MEETING EACH WEEK

It will help coordinate the various meals, chores, and functions of the household. As children get older and start keeping their own schedules, a regular family hour can be valuable to establish contact. It keeps each family member communicating with the others and brings everyone together.

104

MOVE TIME-WASTERS OUT OF THE WAY

We chose to put our entertainment center off-center in our living room and in an enclosed piece of furniture. Why? So that we don't find ourselves automatically turning on the TV, starting a video, or even listening to music. We can do all those things, but we do so by choice, not by impulse when one of us enters the room. We once had our TV on a table at the foot of our bed. We watched more TV and spent less time communicating and sleeping. Now the TV is in a cabinet that must be opened each time. The cabinet helped us become more discretionary with our viewing time.

Someone else suggested putting the TV on a timer that shuts it off after every hour. It serves to make the viewer more aware of how much TV you are watching.

105

CHOOSE THE RIGHT TIME FOR DECISION MAKING

Don't make strategic decisions when you are exhausted, frustrated, or over-whelmed with stress. Fatigue and stress can decrease your ability to make wise choices.

CHAPTER 7

CHOOSING TO SIMPLIFY

Motivation to Last a Lifetime. The title caught my eye because it spoke to my own need. I know how to stay motivated for a day or a week. But a lifetime? When emotional energy wears off, my motivation goes with it.

Motivation experts say we stay motivated when we know that something good will come out of our action—for ourselves, for someone else, or both. The hope of heaven or fear of hell helps motivate us to follow Jesus Christ. The need for unity motivates us to serve our family. The promise of salary, security, and significance motivates us to do our best at work.

So what motivates us to simplify our lives? What are the benefits to cutting back, getting focused, and changing our lifestyles?

THE BOTTOM LINE: Simplifying our lives is the best way to promote overall personal health. That's our motivation for a lifetime.

FIRST: BEWARE OF THE DE-MOTIVATORS

Before looking at the pros of simplifying, a quick warning about the negative forces that will militate against simplifying our schedules, our lifestyles, or even our spiritual commitments. Howard Macy identifies five reasons why we continue living in ways that are overcommitted and unhealthy for our bodies and spirits. He cites:

1) "Overestimating: wanting to deny that we have limitations." We take on more responsibilities than we can handle given our gifts, time, and other commitments.

2) "Pleasing: hoping that the more we do for people the more they will like us." This leads to a frantic, scattered investment of energy because we are always seeking to gain the approval of the last person we spoke with.

3) "Rescuing: running in all directions to help those in need." We burn ourselves out trying to be the remedy to everyone else's problems.

4) "Guilt: refusing to say no because the response we might get from others might cause more guilt than we can deal with."

5) "Smorgasbording: life spreads a buffet before us and we're tempted to take a little of this and a little of that so that we are superficially involved in a host of activities." This in turn leads to spreading thin our energies and resources.[1]

Identifying these tendencies can take us back to the drawing board where we ask ourselves, "What (or where) do I need to cut back to live with the focus and energy that God intends for me?"

THE BENEFITS OF A SIMPLER LIFE

In the lives of others, as well as my own, I have observed at least five benefits of simplifying—all of them contribute to our overall health,

---

1.   Howard R. Macy, "Just Say No," *Discipleship Journal* (Issue 60, 1990), 29–33. Used by permission. All rights reserved.

while others contribute to our ability to serve with greater energy and effectiveness.

SPIRITUAL BENEFITS

When I simplify my life, I sharpen the focus on my relationship with God. Slowing down strengthens my prayer life, allows me to absorb Scripture, and opens my ears to hear God's voice.

Cutting back my busy schedule helps eliminate some of the "noise" in my life, letting me hear God's call to "Be still and know that I am God" (Psalm 46:10). When I respond to Jesus' invitation to bring my weariness to Him, I find the "rest for my soul" that He promised (see Matthew 11:28–30).

In the midst of an economic downturn in his line of work, Joe was laid off by his company. Our Sunday School class began praying for him to find a new job—especially since he had a mortgage to pay and a family of five to feed.

Joe surprised us one Sunday when he told us his layoff was a gift from God: "The time without work has shown me how I was neglecting my development as a person of God." he said. "With more time to pray, think, and read the Scriptures, I am rearranging my priorities. I am looking at issues like career, salaries, and possessions differently. My ambitions and goals are being rearranged, and I am becoming a deeper man. Unemployment put God back at the center of my life."

Joe discovered how hectic schedules and materialistic priorities deflect our desire for God. He had been a victim of what Tony Campolo identifies as an age where consumerism promises us spiritual fulfillment and we "no longer know what spiritual longings really are."[2]

Joe soon was back to work, but he took a job with less responsibility and less pay so he can keep his spiritual priorities straight.

Jean Fleming observes that "unless we purposely slow our pace and narrow our focus, we will miss the marrow of life."[3] This "marrow" of life is to know God and enjoy our relationship with Him; slowing down diminishes the distractions that divert us from His purpose.

When we simplify—taking attention off ourselves and looking to Almighty God—we find refreshment for our spirits and relief from our

2.   Tony Campolo, *Wake Up America!* (Grand Rapids: Zondervan, 1991), 7.

3.   Jean Fleming, "Personal Retreat: A Special Date with God," *Discipleship Journal* (Issue 60, 1990): 34.

tensions. The needs of the world fall under God's responsibility. He ordains us to participate, but our frantic pace implies that God is helpless without our help. He sent us a Messiah (Jesus) so that we can find rest and fulfillment in Him.

Jean Fleming writes,

> A fast-paced life can become an opiate. We seemingly thrive on activity and pressure, and think all is well because we fly along on the adrenaline of frenzy. Not until our engine cuts (through something like sickness, relational breakdown, or unemployment) do we face the sobering realities that inactivity and silence bring. Busyness saps spiritual vitality. . . . Spiritual vitality is possible only when we take the time to let God's presence recharge us.[4]

Simplifying corrects our focus: we put Jesus Christ at the center of our lives and an appropriate lifestyle flows from this spiritual renewal.

---

4.   Ibid., 37

PHYSICAL BENEFITS

Good stewardship relates to our physical bodies as well. Simplifying our lives will contribute to our physical health and make us better stewards.

In his book, *Staying Well*, Richard Ecker looks at the stress, lifestyle, and eating habits of the average American and describes "why the good life is so bad for you."[5] He notes that a hectic life, a poor diet, and a sedentary lifestyle promote poor health.

If we slow down, we can more easily stay away from "fast food," eat less junk food, and exercise more often. By simplifying my life I have lowered my blood pressure and eliminated tension headaches. Regular exercise has sharpened my ability to think and enabled me to be more productive in my work.

RELATIONAL BENEFITS

Michael Morris, curate of Saint Mark's Episcopal Church in Geneva, Illinois, summarized relational struggles this way; "Most live in their

---

5.   Subtitle to Richard E. Ecker's, *Staying Well* (Downers Grove: Inter-Varsity Press, 1984).

own isolated boxes in the suburbs, a thousand miles away from family, in communities in which they feel no roots. They are plagued by loneli-ness—yet driven by demanding jobs and compet-ing family needs."[6]

Something must change if we want to lose our loneliness. A simpler lifestyle allows us to build our primary relationships. Over the years, we have dedicated a lot of time to overseas ministry, and the time away from home has often led to our finding friends to house-sit.

One consistent complaint from the people who have stayed in our home relates to our technol-ogy. At one point, they complained that we had no dishwasher, video player or CD-player. At this writing, the complaints might be because we have no DVD or MP3 players. No flat-screen TV? No high-definition cable? How do we survive?

Our explanation has always remained the same: we have nothing against such entertain-ment or gadgetry, but we want to eliminate obsta-cles to spending quality time together. Watching the TV or movies renders us passive spectators.

---

6.   Quoted by Paula Rinehart in "The Pivotal Generation," *Christianity Today* (October 6, 1989): 24.

We prefer to engage in face-to-face conversation rather than be distracted from each other.

Millard Fuller was a millionaire lawyer by 29. He was the picture of success, but his marriage was falling apart. Together, he and his wife identified how the quest for "things" had left them burned out and spiritually dead. They committed to serving the poor and oppressed through Habitat for Humanity and their marriage was saved. Millard explains, "We were giving up a whole way of life that was killing us."[7]

Howard Macy writes, "Nobody makes me take on the overload of commitments that destroy any reasonable schedule and drain my energy."[8] In the same way, nobody will make me cut back to focus on my network of relationships. I must decide. If we desire to give priority to our friends, spouses, and children, something else in our schedules must go.

---

7.   Tony Campolo tells this story in *Wake Up America!* (Grand Rapids; Zondervan, 1991),105.

8.   Howard R. Macy, "Just Say No," *Discipleship Journal* (Issue 60, 1990), 29. Used by permission. All rights reserved.

ECONOMIC BENEFITS

A simpler lifestyle is a freer lifestyle. Living debt-free delivers us from the fear of the next credit card invoice or that dreaded call from a collection agency. Downsizing our homes, our budgets, and our expectations can release us from the self-created pressures to own, buy, or achieve.

In addition to freeing us personally, a simpler lifestyle enables us to serve others. We can respond more liberally to those in need because our finances are not so stretched. We become more available to listen to and care for a friend in need because we have the time.

GLOBAL BENEFITS

We live in a global village that is becoming smaller each day. Global interdependency calls us, as the people of God, to look at ourselves differently.

A simplified life helps us relate to a world of diminishing resources. If I lower my consumption of natural resources, I am acting more responsibly as a world citizen. I have more to give to those in need—both locally and internationally.

Experts predict that the resources of our world cannot sustain the affluent Western lifestyle. Simplifying our lives allows us to strengthen our sense of being God's people in a needy world.

GO FOR IT!

In the movie *Curly Sue*, a wealthy, ruthless lawyer's perspective is rearranged by her encounter with homeless people. She sees the world in a new light, starts using her resources differently, and eventually uses her legal expertise to defend a homeless child—eventually abandoning her pursuit of being a partner in a prestigious law firm in order to defend the rights of the homeless.

In a poignant moment when she is resigning from her law firm, the boss comments, "You're the last lawyer I would have expected to choose to leave based on the 'quality of life' thing."

She chose a life with meaning and love over a life of greed and professional success. And that's the choice we make when we cut back. We go against the culture where "having it all" has become a goal, if not a god.

Where will we find a lifetime of motivation to simplify our lives? We will find it in the positive effects simplifying has on us and on those we touch.

WAYS TO SIMPLIFY
YOUR LIFE

106. Pray for change

106

PRAY FOR CHANGE

Pray about every choice you make as a result of this book. External exercises to simplify must be complemented by inner spiritual change to help us deal with the clutter within. Howard Macy writes, "No doubt over-committed people find help in better time management techniques, as I have, but many of them will use their newfound skills to pack more obligation into their lives rather than to step back from the madcap pace. As they get better, they also get worse, mostly because they are ignoring causes while dealing with symptoms."[9]

---

9.   Howard R. Macy, "Just Say No," *Discipleship Journal* (Issue 60, 1990), 29. Used by permission. All rights reserved.

10 BIBLICAL PRINCIPLES TO HELP FOSTER A WORLD CHRISTIAN LIFESTYLE[1]

While we can exhort and encourage each other to love and good deeds regarding a generous life-style, the Scriptures guide us through principles, and each person, family, and fellowship must ulti-mately wrestle with our own lifestyle choices based on these biblical guidelines. Here are ten that we use to guide our lives.

---

1. These ten principles originally appeared in *Discipleship Journal*, Vol. 25, No. 4 (July/August 2006), 44.

1) *Responsibility:* "to whom much is given . . . much will be required" (Luke 12:48 NKJV). We are each responsible before God with how we manage what he entrusts to us.

2) *Judgment:* "Do not judge or you too will be judged" (Matthew 7:1ff). When it comes to lifestyle issues, we must be careful to suspend our desire to justify ourselves by condemning those whose lifestyle is more affluent. Leave their judgment to God.

3) *Compassion:* we must not let our hearts get hardened when we see others in need (see 1 John 3:16–18). Maintain a heart of compassion. Don't get so numbed by the crises, poverty, or need of our world that we no longer feel anything and we let apathy (literally, "no feeling") creep in. Matthew 25:31–46 reminds of the severity of judgment on those whose hearts became callused and indifferent to the poor. To build compassion, we're reminded to see every poor or isolated or disadvantaged person as Jesus himself.

4) *Celebration*: "For everything God created is good . . . if it is received with thanksgiving" (1 Timothy 4:4–5). There is a time for feasting as well as a time for fasting. God gives us a life filled with joy; the "world-

Christian lifestyle" does not mean a life of guilt.

5) *Generosity:* "God loves a cheerful giver" (2 Corinthians 9:6–7). God loves to see us be generous towards others, and he promises greater fruitfulness to those who "sow generously."

6) *Freedom from debt:* "Let no debt remain outstanding, except the continuing debt to love one another" (Romans 13:8). God doesn't want us to give our freedom over to indebtedness, because, as Proverbs 22:7 reminds us, "the borrower is servant to the lender."

7) *A soldier's discipline:* Paul describes Christians as soldiers in active service (2 Timothy 2:4–5). The discipline of saying no to our cravings, addressing and defeating the consumerism of our age, and identifying the lies in marketing (i.e., reminding ourselves that a new car will not bring satisfaction or that impulse buying will enslave us, not free us) doesn't earn God's love. He already loves us. However, we say "no" because we want to grow, and we do not want to be "mastered" by something other than Jesus Christ (1 Corinthians 6:12).

8) *Simplicity*: "give me neither poverty nor riches" (Proverbs 30:7–9). The concept of living simply appears throughout the Scriptures. We should live with the simple faith of a child, and with God-empowered simple desires that can be content regardless of the circumstances (see Philippians 4:11–13).

9) *Sacrifice*: we are urged to imitate "the grace of our Lord Jesus Christ, that though he was rich, yet for your sakes he became poor so that you through his poverty might become rich" (2 Corinthians 8:9). Giving at personal expense is exemplified in Jesus and commended throughout the Scriptures.

10) *Intimacy*: "I have called you by name; you are mine" (Isaiah 43:1). In all of our life situations, God notices. What we do in terms of giving, or cutting back a materialistic lifestyle or choosing simplicity might not be world-changing or globally significant, but the God who knows every sparrow who falls will know when we intentionally choose to bring our lifestyles more in line with his global purposes.

RESOURCES FOR SIMPLIFYING YOUR LIFE

Rather than suggest a host of books to follow up on this topic—which could add to your sense of being overwhelmed—consider these five to challenge your thinking.

Craig Blomberg. *Neither Poverty nor Riches: A Biblical Theology of Material Possessions.* Downers Grove, IL: Inter Varsity Press, 2001.

Paul Borthwick. *How to Be a World-Class Christian.* Colorado Springs: Authentic, 2003.

Henry Cloud and John Townsend. *Boundaries: When*

to Say Yes, When to Say No To Take Control of Your Life. Grand Rapids: Zondervan, 1992.

Ron Sider. *Rich Christians in an Age of Hunger.* Nashville: Thomas Nelson, 2005.

Tom and Christine Sine. *Living on Purpose: Finding God's Best for Your Life.* Grand Rapids: Baker, 2001.

Richard Swenson. *Margin: Restoring Emotional, Physical, Financial and Time Reserves To Overloaded Lives.* Colorado Springs: NavPress, 2004.